Understanding Relational Database Query Languages

Understanding Relational Database Query Languages

Suzanne W. Dietrich

Arizona State University

An Alan R. Apt Book

Prentice Hall
Upper Saddle River, NJ 07458

Library of Congress Cataloging-in-Publication Data

Cip Data on file

Vice President and Editorial Director of ECS: *Marcia Horton*
Publisher: *Alan R. Apt*
Associate Editor: *Toni D. Holm*
Editorial Assistant: *Amy K. Todd*
Vice President and Director of Production and Manufacturing, ESM: *David W. Riccardi*
Executive Managing Editor: *Vince O'Brien*
Managing Editor: *David A. George*
Production Editor: *Lakshmi Balasubramanian*
Director of Creative Services: *Paul Belfanti*
Art Director: *Jayne Conte*
Cover Designer: *Bruce Kenselaar*
Art Editor: *Adam Velthaus*
Manufacturing Manager: *Trudy Pisciotti*
Manufacturing Buyer: *Pat Brown*
Marketing Manager: *Jennie Burger*

Prentice-Hall, Inc.
Upper Saddle River, New Jersey 07458

TRADEMARK INFORMATION

Printed in the United States of America

10 9 8 7 6 5 4 3 2 1

ISBN 0130286524

Prentice-Hall International (UK) Limited, *London*
Prentice-Hall of Australia Pty. Limited, *Sydney*
Prentice-Hall Canada Inc., *Toronto*
Prentice-Hall Hispanoamericana, S.A., *Mexico*
Prentice-Hall of India Private Limited, *New Delhi*
Prentice-Hall of Japan, Inc., *Tokyo*
Pearson Education Asia Pte. Ltd., *Singapore*
Editora Prentice-Hall do Brasil, Ltda., *Rio de Janeiro*

To my Jerry and Jeremy

With Love

Contents

Preface

The goal of this book is to help the reader understand relational database query languages, including the industry-standard structured query language (SQL) and the query languages of the popular PC-based database product Microsoft Access. The book also covers the formal languages upon which SQL is based, such as the relational algebra and relational calculus languages. The relational algebra is a procedural language having specific operators to apply to relations for the retrieval of data. Most educators agree that an understanding of relational algebra is *critical* to understanding SQL. The relational calculus languages, like SQL, are declarative query languages, indicating the properties of the data to be retrieved. There are two types of relational calculus query languages: domain relational calculus (DRC), where a variable ranges over a domain or column of a table, and tuple relational calculus (TRC), where a variable ranges over a tuple or row of a table. This book covers the DRC language, because of the use of DRC-like languages for the specification and optimization of data mining techniques and related technologies that integrate database and artificial intelligence. The book covers the TRC language, because the basic SQL query expression is a syntactic variation of an expression in TRC. Again, an understanding of TRC provides a strong foundation for understanding the industry-standard query language SQL.

The book is based on the premise that understanding comes from a wealth of examples and a hands-on approach. The various query languages are explored through not only detailed examples, but also side-by-side comparisons of the languages on various types of queries over several database enterprises. This example-based approach is reinforced by the inclusion of an appendix that describes the WinRDBI educational tool, which is available on the Web. (See Appendix A.)

The WinRDBI educational tool provides a graphical, interactive environment for a hands-on approach to understanding the query languages. The queries marked with a check (√) in the book are provided electronically on the companion website so that the reader can *check* the results of the queries using the tool.

The targeted audience of the book ranges from a student that is enrolled in an introductory database management course to the professional engineer that wants to understand the foundations of SQL. Students in an introductory database management course, which is offered in many disciplines including computer science, computer information systems and industrial engineering, will find this book useful as a supplemental text. However, the book is self-contained, so that it is accessible to the professional engineer faced with using relational database technology. For example, the first chapter of the book includes an introduction to the relational data model, an overview of the conceptual design of a database based on the requirements of an enterprise, and a description of mapping the conceptual design to the relational data model. The assumed prerequisites include the knowledge of set theory and the desire to understand relational database query languages.

CHAPTER GUIDE

1. THE RELATIONAL DATA MODEL
   This chapter is useful to all readers, since it introduces the terminology and notation of the text, and the example enterprise used throughout the book.
2. RELATIONAL ALGEBRA
   Most educators agree that understanding relational algebra is *critical* to understanding *any* relational database query language. The examples presented in this chapter form the basis of the exposition of the other query languages.
3. DOMAIN RELATIONAL CALCULUS
   The relational calculus languages provide the foundation for declarative query languages, such as SQL, that state the properties of the data to be retrieved. The DRC language also forms the foundation of declarative languages used for the integration of database and artificial intelligence technologies. The DRC language uses variables that range over a column of a table. This approach provides practical shortcuts that are not available in its sibling TRC language, where a variable ranges over the row of a table. Most students introduced to the DRC and TRC languages prefer the paradigm offered by DRC, although there are always a few students who prefer the procedural paradigm offered by relational algebra. You are cheerfully invited to read this chapter and the TRC chapter that follows and make up your own mind.
4. TUPLE RELATIONAL CALCULUS
   Since the basic SQL query expression is a syntactic variation of a TRC expression, it is recommended to cover the TRC language before SQL. The TRC chapter introduces tuple variables, which are variables that range over

the tuples or rows of a relation. In SQL, these tuple variables are called *table aliases*, or *range variables*.

5. SQL
   This chapter explores SQL in the context of its mathematical foundations. The basic query expression in SQL is mapped to its equivalent relational algebra expression and its similarity to an expression of the tuple relational calculus language is illustrated. The examples over the working enterprise use basic features of the SQL language to reinforce the relationship between SQL and the formal query languages. For pragmatic reasons, SQL is more powerful than its formal counterparts on which it is based. These additional features of SQL are illustrated by example. Since the SQL standard evolved to provide more than a query language, this chapter also covers the standard's data definition language, data manipulation language, and data control language for integrity and security.
6. CASE STUDIES
   This chapter provides the opportunity for the reader to work through three case studies starting from a requirements description, to its conceptual design, its relational data model implementation, and then a side-by-side comparison of the four query languages using relevant queries over the case study.
7. MICROSOFT ACCESS
   The goal of this chapter is to relate theory to practice by covering the query languages provided by the popular, PC-based database product Microsoft Access.

A. WINRDBI EDUCATIONAL TOOL
   This appendix chapter provides an overview of the WinRDBI educational tool, describing the assumptions of the query languages recognized by the educational tool (relational algebra, domain relational calculus, tuple relational calculus, and SQL).

FOR MORE INFORMATION

The Prentice Hall companion website for this book is at the URL:

`http://www.prenhall.com/dietrich`

The WinRDBI educational tool and the author's website for the book is at the URL:

`http://www.eas.asu.edu/~winrdbi`

An instructor resource CD is available, which contains supporting material for the book including solutions to chapter exercises for WinRDBI.

The author's preferred email address for correspondence regarding the book is:

`swdietrich@asu.edu`

ACKNOWLEDGMENTS

There are many people who are involved in the process of writing and publishing a book. I appreciate the thoughtful guidance in the writing of the book that was provided by the reviewers: Chris Eagle, Ibrahim Imam, William Perrizo, Munindar Singh, Jennifer Widom, and Dawn Wilkins. My thanks to those at Prentice Hall who warmly welcomed me as a member of their family of authors: Alan Apt, Toni Holm, Amy Todd, Lakshmi Balasubramanian, Jennie Burger, Jayne Conte, David George, Vince O'Brien, Cindy Szollose and Jake Warde.

My involvement in the design and development of the WinRDBI educational tool provided the motivation for writing this book. The following students contributed to the development of WinRDBI: Eric Eckert, Changguan Fan, Chien-Ho Ho, Ana Hun, Kevin Piscator, Rick Rankin and Sarah Simons. Rick deserves a special acknowledgment since he maintained the software for some time after he graduated. I also want to thank Amzi!, inc. for their assistance, since WinRDBI utilizes the Amzi! Prolog and Logic Server as the basis of its underlying implementation.

The task of writing a book requires a long-term commitment of time and energy. I want to express my sincere gratitude to my family and friends for the encouragement and understanding.

Chapter 1

The Relational Data Model

Relational databases are a valuable tool for providing solutions to mission-critical applications in industry, especially those involving e-commerce and the World Wide Web. Relational databases provide the conceptual simplicity of modeling information using tables, yet provide the power to handle many different types of application domains. This chapter provides an overview of the relational data model. Specifically, this overview introduces the terminology used in discussing relations and the notation used in this book. To make the technology accessible to a wide range of readers, the chapter includes coverage of taking a description of the requirements of an enterprise to its representation as relational tables. The requirements are modeled conceptually using a graphical notation, called the Entity-Relationship conceptual data model. This conceptual design is then mapped to relational tables. The resulting relational design, known as a schema, represents the requirements of the enterprise by providing the description of tables in which the data are stored. Assuming that the tables store valid data, the next step in building a database application is effective retrieval of the data from the tables. The languages that provide a framework for retrieving information from a database are called query languages. Understanding the various query languages is the focus of this book.

1.1 INTRODUCTION

The relational data model is widely accepted because of its conceptual simplicity and its theoretical foundations. This section (hopefully painlessly) provides an introduction to this theoretical basis. The conceptual simplicity of a relation is based on concepts with which most of us are familiar, such as a table data structure having rows and columns or a file having records and fields. Table 1.1 provides a summary of the terminology used for relations versus a table or a file. A *relation* corresponds to a table or a file. The rows of a table or records of a file are called the *tuples* of a relation. The names of the columns or fields are called *attributes*. The *degree*, or *arity*, of a relation corresponds to its number of columns. The term *cardinality* refers to the number of tuples or rows in the table.

TABLE 1.1 Summary of terminology correspondence.

Relation	Table	File
tuple	row	record
attribute	column name	field
degree or arity	number of columns	number of fields
cardinality	number of rows	number of records

A relation is described by its schema or intension. For example, `r(a1, a2, ..., an)` describes a relation named `r` having n attributes named `a1, a2, ..., an`, respectively. Each attribute `ai` has an associated domain of basic or atomic values. An atomic value is one that is not divisible into smaller components. In the relational data model, a composite attribute cannot be defined. For example, to store the name of a person in a table, two attributes of type string must be used, one each for first name and last name. The atomic-valued domain is an underlying assumption of the relational data model.

Formally, an instance or extension of a relation `r` having schema `r(a1, a2, ..., an)` is a set of n-tuples. Each n-tuple is an ordered list of n-values, where the ith value corresponds to the value of the ith attribute `ai`, which is an element from the domain associated with `ai` or a null value. A null value designates that the value of that attribute in the tuple is unknown. Figure 1.1 shows a sample instance of an employee relation having schema `employee(eID, eLast, eFirst, eTitle, eSalary)`.

Since a relation extension is a set of tuples and a mathematical set is defined as an unordered collection with no duplicate elements, there is no implied ordering between the tuples in a relation, and there can be no duplicate tuples. Two tuples are duplicates if they have the same value for all of their attributes. For the `employee` table, the no-duplicate-tuples constraint indicates that no two tuples can have the same values for all of the attributes: `eID, eLast, eFirst, eTitle`, and `eSalary`. However, for the employee schema, the `eID` attribute is assumed to be a unique employee identifier such that no two employee tuples can have the same value for the `eID` attribute. For a relation, a uniqueness constraint can be defined based on some of the attributes in the relation's schema.

Relation Schema and Uniqueness

Up to this point, a relation schema is described by a tupling of the relation's attributes, which is typically denoted by the use of parentheses (e.g., `r(a1, a2, ..., an)`). When only the names of the attributes of a relation are of interest and not the ordering of the attributes within the tuple of the relation, a relation's schema can also be described using set notation to refer to the set of attributes in the schema. Typically, the curly braces ({and}) are used to surround the elements of a set. By convention, let `R` represent the set of attributes for a relation `r`. Therefore, `R` = {`a1`, `a2`, ..., `an`} for the relation schema `r(a1, a2, ..., an)`. For the `employee` table, `EMPLOYEE` = {`eID, eLast, eFirst, eTitle, eSalary`}.

`employee`

eID	eLast	eFirst	eTitle	eSalary
222	Last222	First222	Software Engineer	51, 722
333	Last333	First333	Sr Software Engineer	60, 333
666	Last666	First666	Coach	66, 666
999	Last999	First999	Manager	100, 999
		⋮		

Figure 1.1 Sample instance of the `employee table`.

Dot notation is used to access the value of an attribute of a tuple. For example, given a tuple t over a relation having schema `r(a1, a2, ..., an)`, t.`ai` references the value of attribute `ai` of the tuple t. Consider extending this dot notation to reference the value of multiple attributes resulting in a tuple of attribute values. Let t be a tuple over a relation having schema `r(a1, a2, ..., an)`, then t.(`ai, ..., aj`) = (t.`ai`, ..., t.`aj`) where {`ai`, ..., `aj`} ⊆ `R`. If {`ai`, ..., `aj`} ⊂ `R`, then t.(`ai, ..., aj`) references some of the attributes of the tuple t. If {`ai`, ..., `aj`} = `R`, then t.(`ai, ..., aj`) references the entire tuple.

The no-duplicate-tuples constraint built-in to the definition of a relation as a set of tuples can be restated as follows: Let t1 and t2 be distinct tuples over a relation having schema `r(a1, a2, ..., an)`; then t1.(`a1, a2, ..., an`) ≠ t2.(`a1, a2, ..., an`). Thus, the no-duplicate-tuples constraint is a default uniqueness constraint for a relation.

A *superkey* for a relation having schema `r(a1, a2, ..., an)` is defined to be any set of attributes {`ai, ..., aj`} satisfying {`ai, ..., aj`} ⊆ R such that for any two distinct tuples t1 and t2, t1.(`ai, ..., aj`) $\neq$ t2.(`ai, ..., aj`). A superkey defines a uniqueness constraint for a relation, but a superkey may contain more attributes than necessary to uniquely identify a tuple. For example, `EMPLOYEE` is a superkey of `employee(eID, eLast, eFirst, eTitle, eSalary)`, but `eID`, by itself, uniquely identifies an employee tuple. A minimal superkey, a superkey for which no subset forms a superkey, is called a *candidate key*. Therefore, `eID` is a candidate key of `employee`, whereas `EMPLOYEE` is not a candidate key, since {`eID`} $\subseteq$ `EMPLOYEE` and `eID` is a superkey.

Candidate keys are designated on a relation schema using an underline (e.g., `employee(eID, eLast, eFirst, eTitle, eSalary)`). A relation may have several candidate keys. For example, if it can be assumed that the combination of the `eLast` and `eFirst` attributes uniquely identifies an employee, then {`eLast, eFirst`} and {`eID`} are each a candidate key. The primary candidate key used to uniquely identify tuples in a table is called the *primary key*. In addition to specifying a uniqueness constraint, a primary key implies that the value of the attributes forming the primary key cannot be null.

Relational Database Schema and Referential Integrity

A relational database does not consist of a single relation, but a collection of relations that are logically related. Therefore, the schema of a relational database is a set of relation schemas, along with constraints that define the relationships between the relations. Each relation name must be unique within a relational database schema. An attribute name is unique within a relation schema.

The most common logical relationship between relations in a relational database schema is given by referential integrity constraints, where an attribute in one table references an attribute value in another table. For example, consider a relational database consisting of the `employee` relation and a `title` relation, where the relation schema `title(tTitle, tMinSalary, tMaxSalary)` denotes the possible titles for employees and the attributes `tMinSalary` and `tMaxSalary` denote the minimum and maximum salaries for the given title. Let the value of the `eTitle` attribute of the `employee` table reference the primary key `tTitle` of the `title` table, indicating that the value of `eTitle` is either null or appears in the `tTitle` attribute for some tuple in the `title` table. The `eTitle` attribute is called a *foreign key*.

An attribute or set of attributes is a foreign key of a referencing table `r1` if it references the primary key of the referenced table `r2`. Thus, the foreign key of `r1` and the primary key of `r2` must have the same domain. The referential integrity constraint requires that if the value of the foreign key attributes in `r1` is not null, then it is equal to the value of the primary key attributes of some tuple in `r2`. In the context of a single attribute as a foreign key, let `f` denote the foreign key attribute of `r1` and `p` denote the primary key attribute of `r2`, then for a tuple t1 ranging over r1 either t1.`f` = null or there exists a tuple t2 in `r2` such that t1.`f` = t2.p. Figure 1.2

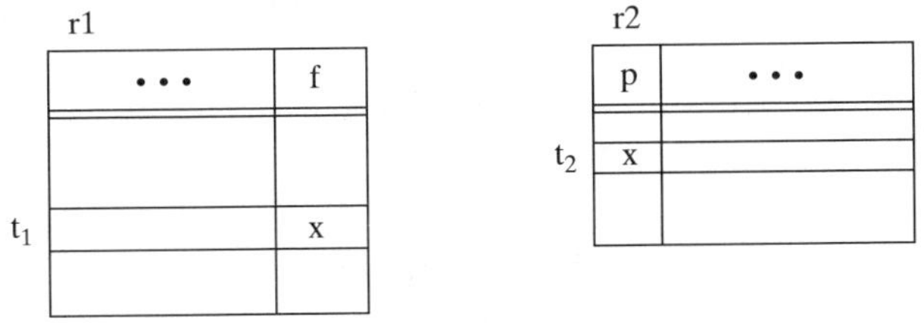

Foreign key r1.f references primary key r2.p

Figure 1.2 Referential integrity constraint.

provides a pictorial representation of this referential integrity constraint, indicating that the nonnull value for the foreign key attribute `f` in `r1` must appear as a value for the primary key attribute `p` in `r2`.

There are other constraints between relations in a database that must be explicitly supported by the database application. For example, the salary of an employee must fall within the salary ranges specified for the employee title. This is an explicit constraint that ideally is defined using a declarative constraint specification language, making the database responsible for enforcing the constraint. Otherwise, the database application programmer must check the constraint in any code that affects the employee's salary, title or salary ranges.

1.2 CONCEPTUAL DESIGN

The process of designing a relational database schema can be quite complex. One of the first steps in the design process is to gather the requirements of the enterprise. A conceptual data model acts as a bridge between the requirements document and the implementation. Consider the following brief requirements of an enterprise on employee training:

> A company wants to maintain a database on the training courses that it provides to its employees. Each training course is offered to fit within a technology area deemed important by the company for its strategic directions. Each technology area has an employee identified as its lead, who has the responsibility to maintain a Web page on the company's intranet to provide its employees with the current state of this technology area. The employees that took a training course on a given date are maintained in the database.

Does this description provide enough information to design the database? It probably does not, but it does provide a good starting point. You should be thinking of questions to ask your user:

- What characteristics do you want the database to maintain about employees, training courses and technology areas?
- Must a technology area have an employee lead? Can an employee lead more than one technology area?

- Does a training course have to be classified in one of the technology areas? Can it be classified in more than one technology area?
- Can an employee take the same training course more than once?

The answers that your user provides regarding how their company works will guide the database design. In this scenario, assume the following:

- The characteristics of an employee include a unique employee identification number, a last name, a first name, a title, and a salary. An employee can be the lead of at most one technology area. An employee can take many training courses, but can take a given training course at most once.
- The characteristics of a training course include a unique course identity, a title and the length of the course in hours. A training course must be classified within exactly one of the identified technology areas. Many employees can take a training course, and the date that an employee takes a training course must be maintained.
- The characteristics of a technology area include a unique area identity, a title, and the universal resource locator (URL) of the Web page for the technology area. A technology area must have exactly one employee lead, but can have many associated training courses.

The goal of a conceptual data model is to capture the constraints of the enterprise at a higher level of abstraction than the level of implementation. The Entity-Relationship (ER) conceptual data model uses a graphical notation to represent this abstraction through ER diagrams.

Figure 1.3 gives an ER diagram for the EMPLOYEE TRAINING enterprise. An entity represents the type of an object of interest in the enterprise. In the working example, the entities are employee, training course, and technology area. In an ER diagram, a rectangular box denotes an entity, and the name of the entity is displayed within the rectangle.

An entity is described by its characteristics, which are called attributes. Attribute names are enclosed within ovals that are linked to the entity it is describing. The employee entity has attributes `eID`, `eName`, `eTitle` and `eSalary`. The attributes `eID`, `eTitle`, and `eSalary` are simple attributes. The attribute `eName` is a composite attribute, which consists of the simple attributes `eLast` and `eFirst`. An attribute is assumed to have a single value, unless it is denoted by a double oval, which indicates that the attribute can have multiple values. Although not included in this example, a multivalued `eSkills` attribute could be defined that represents the skill set of an employee. An attribute whose name is underlined is a key attribute, indicating that the value of this attribute uniquely identifies an entity instance. In the EMPLOYEE TRAINING enterprise, each entity has a key attribute corresponding to the unique identity for that entity.

A relationship is an association between entities. The name of a relationship is displayed within a diamond that is linked to the entities involved in the relationship.

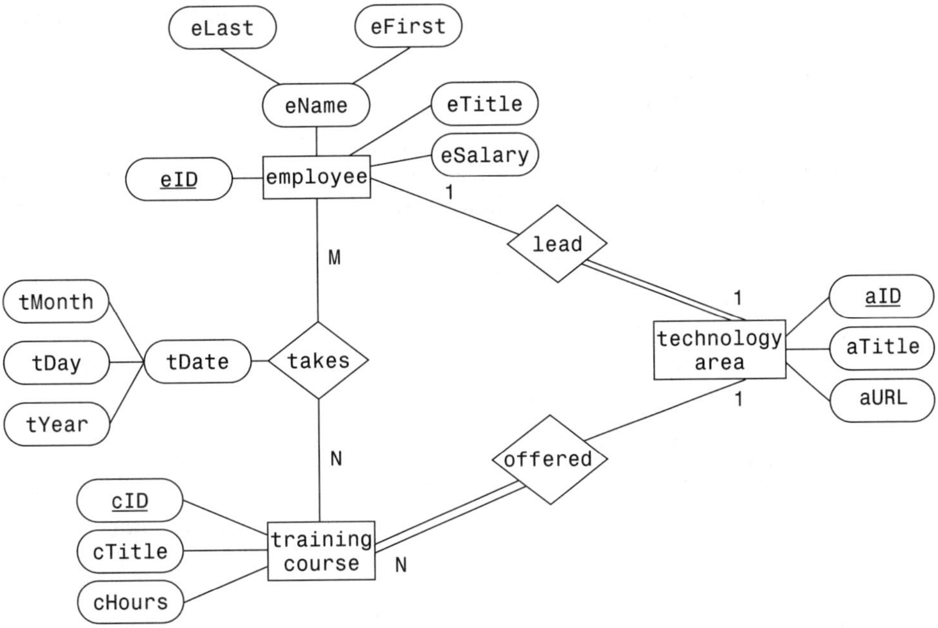

Figure 1.3 Employee Training Entity-Relationship diagram.

Binary relationships, which involve two entities, are the most common type of relationship encountered in the conceptual database design process. The edges linking entities to relationships are annotated to describe the cardinality ratio of the relationship. A cardinality ratio, such as 1:1 (one to one), 1:N (one to many)/N:1 (many to one), M:N (many to many), indicates constraints on the relationship. In the working example, the lead relationship has a 1:1 cardinality ratio, because an employee can lead at most one technology area and exactly one employee must lead a technology area. The offered relationship has a 1:N cardinality ratio, since a training course must be classified within one of the identified technology areas and a technology area can have many associated training courses. The takes relationship has a M:N cardinality ratio because an employee can take many training courses and many employees take a training course.

Cardinality ratios represent a constraint on the number of times that the entities may be involved in the relationship. ER diagrams also provide for the specification of a *participation constraint*, indicating whether a given instance of an entity is required to participate in an instance of the relationship. The participation constraint is denoted by the edge linking the entity to the relationship. A single edge denotes a *partial participation* constraint of the entity in the relationship. A given instance of an entity may participate in the relationship but it is not required to participate. For example, the participation of an employee in the role of a lead in a technology area is partial since an employee may or may not lead a technology area. A double edge denotes a *total participation* of the entity in the relationship.

A given instance of an entity must participate in the relationship. For example, the participation of a technology area in the lead relationship is total, since a technology area must have an employee lead.

There is still a constraint of the EMPLOYEE TRAINING enterprise that has not been discussed in the context of the ER diagram of Figure 1.3: "An employee can take many training courses, but can take a given training course at most once." The cardinality of the takes relationship must be M:N, since an employee can take many training courses and a training course is taken by many employees. The takes relationship has a composite attribute `tDate`, consisting of the month, day, and year that the employee takes the training course. The single-valued characteristic of the `tDate` attribute of the takes relationship implies the constraint limiting an employee to take a specific course once. Otherwise, the `tDate` attribute should be multivalued, representing the dates that an employee took the training course.

There are, however, instance-level constraints that cannot be easily captured at the level of abstraction provided by ER diagrams, including domain constraints and some explicit constraints of the enterprise. Domain constraints limit the value of an attribute to a specific domain. Consider a domain constraint on `eTitle`, which would limit the title of an employee to be only those employee titles within the company. Some explicit constraints of an enterprise can only be enforced by the application code at the implementation level. As an example of such an explicit constraint, consider adding a constraint to the EMPLOYEE TRAINING enterprise that would require an employee lead to have taken at least one training course in the technology area that they lead. Although the ER diagram cannot represent all constraints, there are other constraints that can be captured by ER diagrams and their enhancements for object-oriented modeling that are beyond the scope of this book.

The ER conceptual data model provides, at a glance, a graphical representation of most of the constraints of an enterprise that would otherwise be hidden in the textual description of the requirements of the enterprise. The next section covers a heuristic algorithm for mapping ER diagrams to the relational data model that results in a correct representation of the enterprise at the implementation level.

1.3 MAPPING TO TABLES

Once the conceptual design of the enterprise is complete, the next step is the design of the enterprise within the implementation data model. The mapping of the ER diagram to relational tables is guided by a set of rules. These rules are first illustrated using the abstract entities and relationships of Figures 1.4 and 1.5. Then the rules are applied to the EMPLOYEE TRAINING ER diagram of Figure 1.3.

Figure 1.4(a) contains an entity `e` having a key attribute `eKey`, a composite attribute `eCompositeAttr` consisting of the simple attributes `eSimple1` and `eSimple2`, a single-valued attribute `eSingleValuedAttr`, and a multivalued attribute `eMultiValuedAttr`. The entity `e` is mapped to a table with the same name where the single-valued attributes and the simple attributes of composite attributes are

(a)

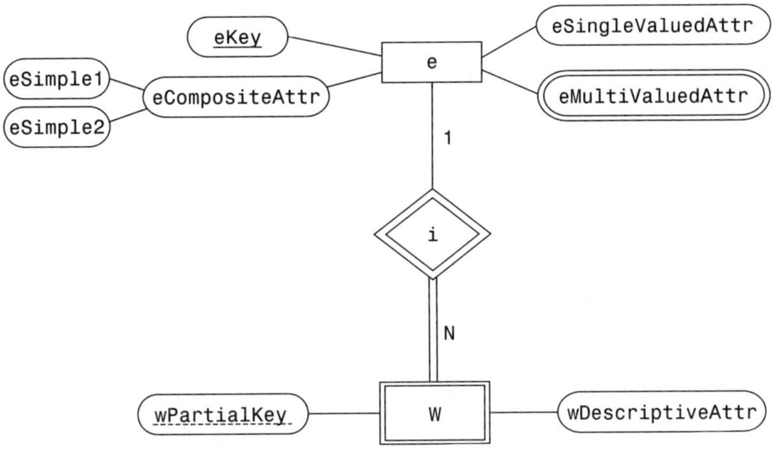

(b)

```
e(eKey, eSingleValuedAttr, eSimple1, eSimple2)
eMulti(eKey, eMultiValuedAttr)
w(eKey, wPartialKey, wDescriptiveAttr)
```

Figure 1.4 Mapping entities to tables: (a) An abstract ER diagram illustrating entities and attributes, and (b) Its mapping to a relational schema.

included as attributes of the table:

e(eKey, eSingleValuedAttr, eSimple1, eSimple2)

Since the eKey attribute uniquely identifies an instance of the entity e, the attribute eKey also forms the key of the table e.

Since the domain of attributes in a relational table must be atomic valued, a multivalued attribute of an entity cannot be directly included in the table for the entity. A separate table is created for each multivalued attribute having as attributes the key of the entity and the multivalued attribute. The table eMulti is created for the multivalued attribute eMultiValuedAttr of the entity e:

eMulti(eKey, eMultiValuedAttr)

Since each entity instance can have multiple values of eMultiValuedAttr, the key for the table eMulti is a composite key consisting of eKey and eMultiValuedAttr.

Up to this point, there has been an implicit assumption that each entity contains a key attribute corresponding to the unique identity for that entity. However, not all entities in an enterprise are guaranteed to have a set of attributes that uniquely identifies that entity across the entire enterprise. The canonical example in an extended employee database is the dependents of an employee. Descriptive attributes for a dependent typically include first name, date of birth, and sex. None

(a)

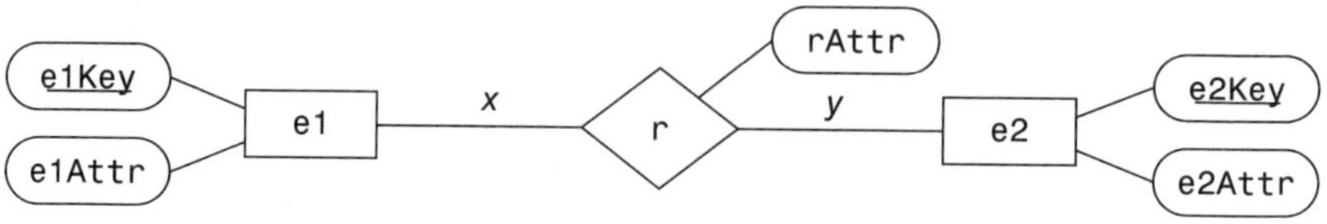

(b)

Cardinality Ratio x : y	Heuristic Design	Alternative Design
1 : 1	e1(e1Key, e1Attr) e2(e2Key, e2Attr) r(e1Key, e2Key, rAttr)	e1(e1Key, e1Attr) e2(e2Key, e2Attr, e1Key, rAttr) assumes that e2 has total participation in r
1 : N	e1(e1Key, e1Attr) e2(e2Key, e2Attr) r(e1Key, e2Key, rAttr)	e1(e1Key, e1Attr) e2(e2Key, e2Attr, e1Key, rAttr)
M : N	e1(e1Key, e1Attr) e2(e2Key, e2Attr) r(e1Key, e2Key, rAttr)	—

Figure 1.5 Mapping relationships to tables: (a) An abstract ER diagram illustrating a binary relationship, and (b) Its mapping to a relational schema based on cardinality ratio.

of these attributes or combination thereof can uniquely identify a dependent in the enterprise, since it is possible that there are two dependents in the database for two different employees that have the same first name, date of birth, and sex. However, the first name and date of birth should uniquely identify a dependent for a given employee. The dependent entity is called a *weak* entity and can be identified by its *partial key* given by first name and date of birth for a given employee.

The abstract ER diagram of Figure 1.4(a) contains a weak entity w, which is denoted by a double rectangle on the ER diagram. The weak entity has a *partial key* or *discriminator*, called wPartialKey, which is an attribute or combination of attributes that uniquely identifies the entity within its *identifying owner*. ER diagrams indicate the partial key by underlining the attribute name by a dashed line. The *identifying owner* is designated by its participation with the weak entity in an *identifying relationship*, which is denoted by a double diamond on the ER diagram. In Figure 1.4(a), the identifying relationship i associates the weak entity w with its identifying owner e. A weak entity has total participation, indicated by the double edge, in its identifying relationship, since it must participate in this relationship to be uniquely identified in the enterprise. A weak entity w is mapped to its own table of the same name, containing its attributes and the key attribute of its identifying owner:

w(eKey, wPartialKey, wDescriptiveAttr)

The key of the table w is formed by the combination of the key of its identifying owner eKey and the partial key of the weak entity wPartialKey.

Entities that have attributes to uniquely identify the entity across the entire enterprise are called *strong* entities. Figure 1.4(b) summarizes the mapping of the abstract ER diagram of Figure 1.4(a), illustrating both strong and weak entities along with composite and multivalued attributes.

Figure 1.5(a) contains an abstract ER diagram denoting a binary relationship r between two abstract entities e1 and e2. The general approach for mapping relationships creates a table r for each relationship r. The key attributes of the entities involved in the relationship and the descriptive attributes of the relationship, if any, are included as the attributes of the corresponding table:

r(e1Key, e2Key, rAttr)

The key of the table r depends on the cardinality ratio of the relationship, which is indicated by an abstract specification of x and y on the edges associating the relationship r to its entities e1 and e2 on the ER diagram of Figure 1.5(a).

A cardinality ratio of 1:1 indicates that an entity instance of e1 is related to at most one instance of entity e2 and an entity instance of e2 is related to at most one instance of entity e1. Therefore, either attribute e1Key or e2Key uniquely identifies an instance of the relationship, which is given by the table r. Since each attribute forms a key of table r, each attribute is underlined separately:

r(e1Key, e2Key, rAttr)

There is an alternative approach for the mapping of a relationship having a 1:1 cardinality ratio. Instead of creating a separate table for r, the key attributes of one side of the relationship r with the descriptive attributes of r are included in a table corresponding to one of the entities involved in the relationship. The decision of which table to modify depends on the participation constraint of the entity in the relationship. In Figure 1.5, let entity e2 have total participation in the relationship r. The alternative design includes the e1Key and rAttr attributes in the table for e2:

e2(e2Key, e2Attr, e1Key, rAttr)

Since entity e2 has total participation in the relationship r, an instance of e2 must be related to exactly one instance of entity e1. If both entities have partial participation in the relationship, the database designer must make an informed choice between the general approach with a separate table for r versus the alternative approach with null values.

A cardinality ratio of 1:N indicates that an entity instance of e1 is related to possibly many instances of entity e2, and an entity instance of e2 is related to at most one instance of entity e1. Therefore, the value of the attribute e2Key uniquely identifies a tuple in the table `r` and is the key of `r`:

`r(e1Key, e2Key, rAttr)`

There is also an alternative design for mapping a relationship having a 1:N cardinality ratio. Instead of creating a table for `r`, include the attributes of the one side of the relationship in the table for the entity on the N-side of the relationship. In Figure 1.5, the table `e2` is modified to include the `e1Key` and `rAttr` attributes:

`e2(e2Key, e2Attr, e1Key, rAttr)`

Note that there is a symmetrical case for a cardinality ratio of N:1, which is not detailed here.

A cardinality ratio of M:N indicates that an entity instance of e1 is related to possibly many instances of entity e2 and an entity instance of e2 is related to possibly many instances of entity e1. Therefore, neither `e1Key` nor `e2Key` can uniquely identify a tuple in the table `r`. However, together `e1Key` and `e2Key` form a composite key of the table `r`:

`r(e1Key, e2Key, rAttr)`

although the actual key for `r` must be ultimately determined in the context of the semantics and constraints of the enterprise being modeled. There is no alternative approach for mapping a relationship having a M:N cardinality ratio. Since each entity instance involved in the relationship is potentially related to many instances of the other entity, a separate table for the relationship `r` must be defined.

The mapping of the abstract ER diagram of Figure 1.5(a) to relational tables is summarized in Figure 1.5(b), illustrating the mapping of an abstract binary relationship `r` having different cardinality ratios.

Table 1.2 summarizes the heuristics for mapping an ER diagram to a relational database schema. Strong entities should be mapped first to facilitate identifying the primary key of an identifying owner when mapping weak entities. The main heuristic for mapping a relationship creates a table for the relationship, which contains the primary key of each entity involved in the relationship and any descriptive attributes of the relationship itself. The primary key of the resulting table ultimately depends on the cardinality ratio of the relationship and the semantics of the enterprise being modeled. However, the previous examples of mapping the abstract ER diagram to a relational database schema discussed the key of the resulting table based on the cardinality ratio and described an alternative design heuristic for relationships with 1:1 and 1:N cardinality ratios. Since the mapping of a weak entity includes the primary key attributes of its identifying owner, identifying relationships are not explicitly mapped since doing so would be redundant. Since the relational model supports only simple types, a multivalued attribute must be mapped to its own table, which includes the primary key of the entity that it is describing.

A relational mapping of the EMPLOYEE TRAINING ER diagram of Figure 1.3 is shown in Figure 1.6, where primary keys are underlined. Table 1.3 summarizes the primary and foreign keys that appear in the EMPLOYEE TRAINING relational database schema. The `employee` table contains the single-valued attributes `eID, eTitle,`

TABLE 1.2 Summary of mapping heuristics.

ER Component	Table	Attributes	Key
strong entity `e`	`e`	simple attributes of `e`	key of `e`
weak entity `w`	`w`	primary key of identifying owner o and simple attributes of w	primary key of o in combination with partial key of w
relationship `r`	`r`	primary key of each entity involved in the relationship and descriptive attributes of `r`	depends on cardinality ratio of `r` and semantics of enterprise
multivalued attribute `m`	`m`	primary key of component c it is describing and the attribute `m`	primary key of `c` in combination with `m`

```
employee(eID, eLast, eFirst, eTitle, eSalary)
technologyArea(aID, aTitle, aURL, aLeadID)
trainingCourse(cID, cTitle, cHours, areaID)
takes(eID, cID, tYear, tMonth, tDay)
```

Figure 1.6 Relational database schema for EMPLOYEE TRAINING enterprise.

TABLE 1.3 Summary of keys in EMPLOYEE TRAINING schema.

Table	Primary Key	Foreign Key	References
`employee`	`eID`	—	—
`technologyArea`	`aID`	`aLeadID`	`employee.eID`
`trainingCourse`	`cID`	`areaID`	`technologyArea.aID`
`takes`	`eID,cID`	`eID`	`employee.eID`
		`cID`	`trainingCourse.cID`

and `eSalary` and the simple attributes `eLast` and `eFirst` of the composite attribute `eName` with key `eID`. The `technologyArea` table includes the mapping of both the technology area entity and the lead relationship. Since a technology area must be related to an employee lead, the key attribute `eID` for employee is included as a foreign key in the `technologyArea` table as the attribute `aLeadID`. Similarly, the `trainingCourse` table maps both the training course entity and the offered relationship. Since a training course must be offered within exactly one technology area, the key attribute `aID` of technology area is included as a foreign key in the `trainingCourse` table as the attribute `areaID`. Since the takes relationship has a M:N cardinality ratio, a separate table `takes` is created having the key attributes of the employee and training course entities and the simple attributes of the composite descriptive attribute `tDate`. The composite key (`eID, cID`) of `takes` uniquely identifies the date the employee took the course. If an employee could take the same training course more than once, then all attributes of the table would form a composite key.

Fortunately, a relational database schema developed from scratch following the approach outlined in this chapter tends to result in a good design. Most database texts cover in detail relational database design theory based on normalization, which characterizes the degrees of redundancy (or lack thereof) in a relational design. Database normalization theory tends to be the most theoretical coverage in a database text and is beyond the scope of this book's introduction to the relational model.

1.4 DATA DEFINITION, STORAGE, AND RETRIEVAL

Once the conceptual and logical database design is complete, the design must be specified in the database product chosen for implementation. Some PC-based products, such as Microsoft Access, provide a graphical user interface (GUI) to facilitate the definition of the database. Most products provide a language for the definition of the database called a *data definition language* (DDL). Both the GUI of Microsoft Access and the data definition component of SQL provide the ability to define tables, including the ability to specify uniqueness and referential integrity constraints. The details of these data definition capabilities will be explored in later chapters.

Once defined, there are various approaches that can be taken to populate or store data in the database. Some PC-based products provide a datasheet view similar to that of a spreadsheet for entering data. Most products provide a tool to aid the user in designing GUIs for their applications using forms. Import capabilities also exist if data need to be loaded from another source. Most products also provide the ability to insert tuples into a table as part of its data manipulation capabilities.

A *data manipulation language* (DML) provides the capability to manipulate the data, including insertion, modification, deletion, and retrieval. Later chapters will explore the data manipulation capabilities of SQL and Microsoft Access. The retrieval component of a DML is called a query language, since a *query* denotes a request for retrieval of information from the database. Here are some possible queries over the EMPLOYEE TRAINING enterprise:

- What training courses are offered in the database technology area?
- Which employees took all of the training courses offered in the database technology area?
- Which employees have not taken any training courses?
- What is the average salary of employees that lead technology areas?

There are many query languages available for the relational data model, including formal, industry-standard, and graphical query languages. The formal languages are based on the mathematical formalism of the relational data model. Relational algebra is a formal, procedural query language having specific operators to apply to relations for retrieving data. Relational calculus is a formal, declarative query language indicating the properties of the data to be retrieved instead of how to retrieve the data. There are two types of relational calculus query languages: domain relational calculus (DRC), where variables range over the domain of an attribute of a relation, and tuple relational calculus (TRC), where variables range over the tuples of a relation. The industry-standard query language SQL is based on TRC. There are also graphical query languages, such as Query by Example (QBE). This book explores the query languages through not only detailed examples, but side-by-side comparisons of the languages on various types of queries.

1.5 SUMMARY

This chapter provided an overview of the relational data model and introduced the notation and terminology used throughout the book. The graphical notation of the ER conceptual data model captured most of the constraints of the enterprise being modeled. The resulting conceptual design formed the basis of the relational database schema using a heuristic approach to map the ER diagram to a collection of tables with uniqueness and referential integrity constraints. Once the relational database is defined and populated, the data can be retrieved from the database using a query language.

SUMMARY OF NOTATION

- The name of relations and attributes are identifiers starting with a lowercase letter.
- A relation schema `r(a1, a2, ..., an)` describes a relation `r` of arity `n`.
- The set of attribute names for a relation schema `r(a1, a2, ..., an)` is denoted by `R` = {`a1, a2, ..., an`}.
- Dot notation is used to access the attributes of a tuple `t` over a relation `r`, e.g., `t.ai` refers to the value of the `ai` attribute of the tuple `t`.

EXERCISES

For more examples of ER diagrams and relational schemas, see the three case studies in Chapter 6. Each case study includes a description of its requirements, its conceptual design using an ER diagram, and its corresponding relational database schema.

1.1 Consider the following requirements for maintaining metadata about the schema of a relational database:

When the schema of a database is defined, either graphically or through the use a DDL, the database must maintain the definition of the database schema for validation purposes. A named database schema consists of several relations. The name of the schema must be unique, and the names of relations are only unique within the database schema. The database also records the degree of the relation. A relation consists of probably several attributes, and attribute names are unique within a relation. Other information recorded about an attribute includes its type and its position. A relation must have a primary key, which consists of one or more of its attributes. A relation may have one or more foreign keys. A foreign key must consist of one or more attributes of the relation in which it appears as a foreign key. A foreign key references the relation in which it appears as a primary key.

(a) Draw an ER conceptual diagram for the enterprise.
(b) State any assumptions that you needed to make in your answer to (a).
(c) State any semantics of the enterprise that cannot be captured by the conceptual design given in (a).

1.2 Consider the following requirements for an online store:

Customers have typical information such as name (last name, first name, and middle initial), address (street, city, state, postal code, and country), phone number, and email. To place an order, customers must be registered users having a unique login name and password. The customer shops the online store by category, where a category has a unique code and description. Each type of item in the online store belongs to exactly one category. An item is described by a unique item number, name, description, and price and has an associated graphic for display on the Web page. Since items may come in different colors and sizes, a customer selects a specific item by also specifying its color and size, which is represented in the database by a code that is unique within the item number. The database also records the current quantity in stock of that item for a given color and size.
The customer places selected items in a shopping cart, specifying the quantity of that item being placed in the cart. There is a unique number associated with the cart along with the date and total price. A shopping cart is associated with exactly one customer, and a customer has exactly one shopping cart. The contents of the shopping cart can be updated until the customer confirms the cart contents by placing an order. The shopping cart is then classified as an order, and the unique identification of the cart is replaced by an order number. Note that a customer can have many orders, but an order is associated with exactly one customer.

(a) Draw an ER conceptual diagram for the enterprise.
(*Hint*: Consider a design that views a shopping cart and an order as the same kind of entity, which has an additional type attribute to distinguish a cart from an order.)
(b) State any assumptions that you needed to make in your answer to (a). Please note that assumptions that you make cannot contradict the description of the enterprise given.
(c) State any semantics of the enterprise that cannot be captured by the conceptual design given in (a).

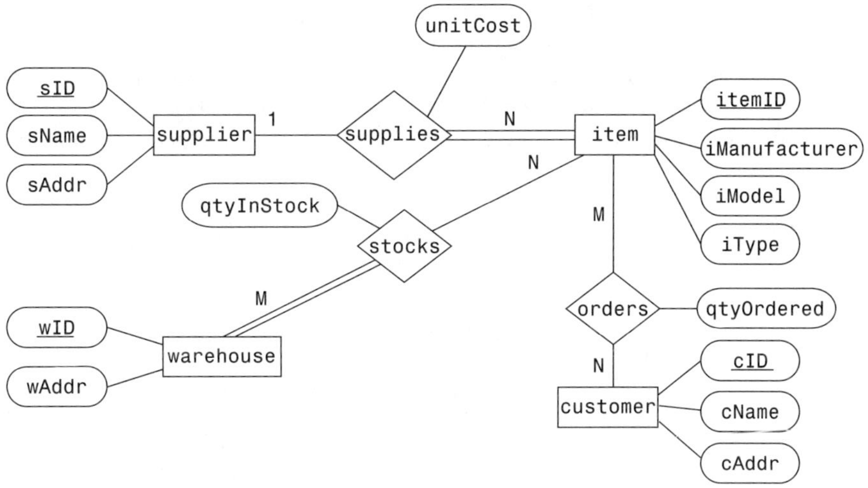

Figure 1.7 WAREHOUSE Entity-Relationship diagram.

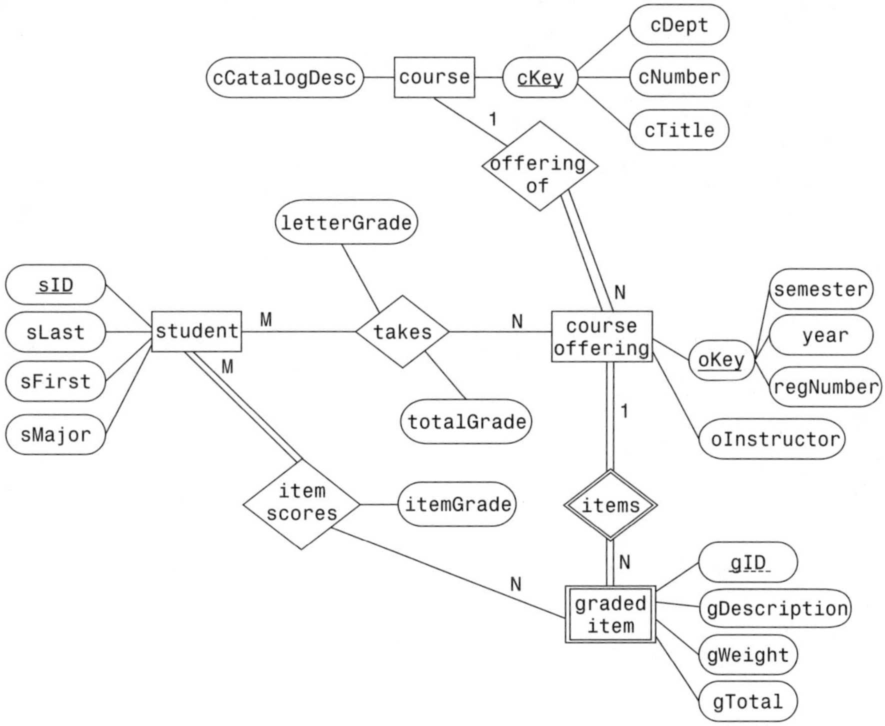

Figure 1.8 GRADEBOOK Entity-Relationship diagram.

1.3 Consider the WAREHOUSE ER diagram of Figure 1.7.

(a) Provide a textual description of the enterprise being represented by the ER diagram.

(b) Map the ER diagram to the relational data model, indicating the primary and foreign keys in the database schema. State any assumptions.

1.4 Answer the questions in Exercise 1.3 for the GRADEBOOK ER diagram of Figure 1.8.

Chapter 2

Relational Algebra

Relational algebra is a procedural query language that applies specific operators to a relation or relations in order to retrieve data. Although the language is formal, it is this formalism of relations as sets of tuples that makes relational algebra straightforward for those familiar with set theory. The fundamental operators characterize the required operations for effectively retrieving data from a relational database. There are additional relational operators that are convenient shorthand notation for frequently used combinations of the fundamental operators. The relational algebra operators are illustrated by detailed queries over the EMPLOYEE TRAINING relational database schema. Since there are multiple ways to write an expression in relational algebra to correctly answer a query, query optimization explores which of the several correct approaches provides a more efficient evaluation.

2.1 FUNDAMENTAL OPERATORS

The fundamental relational algebra operators characterize the required operations for effectively retrieving information from a relational database. Since relations are sets of tuples, most of these operators are familiar to those that know set theory. Some of these operators are unary, meaning that the operator is applied to a single operand relation. The other operators are binary, which are applied to two operand relations. Note that the result of a valid relational algebra expression is itself a relation.

To facilitate a discussion of the operators, Figure 2.1 provides a pictorial definition of the fundamental operators, assuming that relations r and s have the same schema (i.e., $R = S$), but different instances and that relations q and r do not have any attributes in common (i.e., $Q \cap R = \emptyset$).

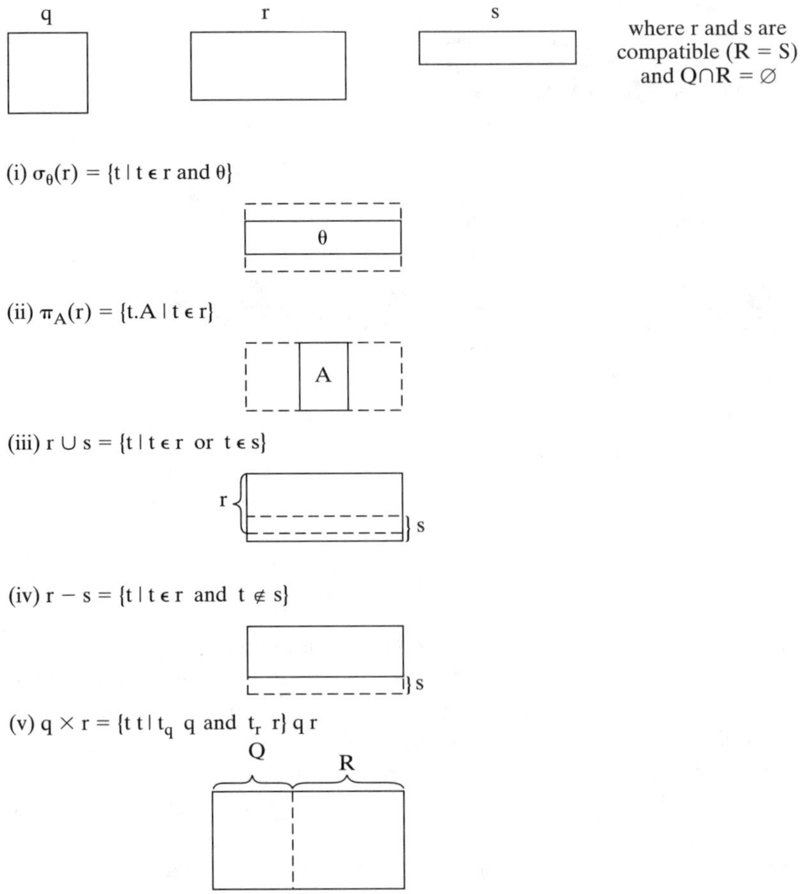

Figure 2.1 Pictorial definition of the fundamental relational algebra operators.

Table 2.1 provides a summary of the schema, degree, and cardinality of each example relational algebra expression in Figure 2.1. Recall that a relation schema gives the attributes of a relation. Table 2.1 represents a relation schema as a set of attributes. Also recall that the degree of a relation is the number of attributes in its schema and that the cardinality of a relation instance is the number of tuples in the table.

UNARY OPERATORS

The unary operators of selection (σ) and projection (π) have a single operand relation and return part of the relation. The result of a selection operation is a horizontal portion of the operand relation and returns a subset of tuples that satisfy the given selection condition. The result of a projection operation is a vertical

TABLE 2.1 Summary of fundamental relational algebra operators.

Relational Algebra Expression	Schema	Degree	Cardinality (upperbound)
$\sigma_\theta(\mathtt{r})$	R	degree(r)	| r |
$\pi_A(\mathtt{r})$	$A \subseteq R$	degree(A)	| r |
$\mathtt{r} \cup \mathtt{s}$	$R = S$	degree(r) = degree(s)	| r | + | s |
$\mathtt{r} - \mathtt{s}$	R	degree(r)	| r |
$\mathtt{q} \times \mathtt{r}$	$Q \cup R$	degree(q) + degree(r)	| q | * | r |

portion of the operand relation and returns a subset of attributes specified in the projection operation.

Selection. The selection operation $\sigma_\theta(\mathtt{r})$ retrieves some of the tuples from the operand relation r that satisfy the selection condition θ:

$$\sigma_\theta(\mathtt{r}) = \{t | t \in \mathtt{r} \text{ and } \theta\}.$$

Typically, the selection condition θ is a boolean combination of comparison terms. The schema and degree of the resulting selection is identical to the operand relation, since the entire tuple is retrieved. The cardinality of the resulting relation ranges from zero, when no tuples of the operand relation satisfy the selection condition, to the cardinality of the operand relation, when all tuples of the operand relation satisfy the selection condition.

Consider a query over the Employee Training enterprise that retrieves those employees whose salary is greater than 100 000:

$\surd Q_\sigma$: $\sigma_{\mathtt{eSalary>100000}}(\mathtt{employee})$;

Projection. The projection operation $\pi_A(\mathtt{r})$ retrieves some of the attributes of a relation as specified by the list of attributes given by the subscript A:

$$\pi_A(\mathtt{r}) = \{t.A | t \in \mathtt{r}\}.$$

For $\pi_A(\mathtt{r})$ to be a valid expression, the set of attributes appearing in A must be a subset of R. The schema and degree of the resulting relation is determined by the projection operation itself. The maximum cardinality of the resulting relation is the same cardinality as the operand relation, which occurs when the key is projected in the resulting attribute list. If the key (or any other unique attribute) of the operand relation is not included in the projection, then there is the potential for duplicate tuples, which are automatically removed from the resulting relation based on the definition of a relation as a set of tuples.

Consider an example query over the Employee Training enterprise that retrieves the last and first names and titles of all employees in the database:

$\surd Q_\pi$: $\pi_{\mathtt{eLast,eFirst,eTitle}}(\mathtt{employee})$;

Binary Operators

The fundamental binary operators are union (∪), difference (−) and cartesian product (×). There are some assumptions that must hold onto the schemas of the operand relations for the valid application of these operators. These assumptions are presented in the context of each operator.

Union. The binary operator union (∪) retrieves the union of the tuples from its operand relations:

$$\mathtt{r} \cup \mathtt{s} = \{t \mid t \in \mathtt{r} \text{ or } t \in \mathtt{s}\}.$$

For this union to make sense, the operand relations must be compatible. The simplest assumption for compatibility is that the relations to be unioned together have identical sets of attribute names and domains.[1] The schema and degree of the resulting union is the same as the operand relations. The maximum cardinality of the result is the sum of the cardinalities of the operand relations, which occurs when the instances of the operand relations do not have any tuples in common. The minimum cardinality occurs when one operand relation is a subset of the other operand relation.

Consider an example query over the EMPLOYEE TRAINING enterprise that retrieves the identification number of employees who are managers or coaches:

$$\sqrt{}\, Q_{\cup} : \pi_{\mathtt{eID}}(\sigma_{\mathtt{eTitle='Manager'}}(\mathtt{employee})) \cup \pi_{\mathtt{eID}}(\sigma_{\mathtt{eTitle='Coach'}}(\mathtt{employee}));$$

This query illustrates that a relation defined by the application of relational algebra operators can be used as an operand relation itself. Since this example query is formed by unioning two selections over the same relation, it can be rephrased using a single selection with a more complicated condition:

$$\sqrt{} \qquad \pi_{\mathtt{eID}}(\sigma_{\mathtt{eTitle='Manager'}\ \mathtt{or}\ \mathtt{eTitle='Coach'}}(\mathtt{employee}));$$

Difference. The binary operator difference (−) retrieves the tuples from the first operand relation that are not in the second operand relation:

$$\mathtt{r} - \mathtt{s} = \{t \mid t \in \mathtt{r} \text{ and } t \notin \mathtt{s}\}.$$

Again, the operand relations of a difference must be compatible using the simplest compatibility assumption. The schema and degree of the resulting difference is the same as the first operand relation. The cardinality of the result $\mathtt{r} - \mathtt{s}$ is denoted $|\mathtt{r} - \mathtt{s}|$. The maximum cardinality of the resulting relation is $|\mathtt{r}|$, which occurs when no tuples from s appear in r. The minimum cardinality of the result is zero, which occurs when the instance of r is a subset of the instance of s.

[1] A more general definition for compatibility can be specified based on attribute position and domain.

Consider an example query over the EMPLOYEE TRAINING enterprise that retrieves the identification number of employees who are managers that have *not* taken any training courses:

$\surd Q_{-}:\quad \pi_{\texttt{eID}}(\sigma_{\texttt{eTitle='Manager'}}(\texttt{employee})) - \pi_{\texttt{eID}}(\texttt{takes});$

Cartesian Product. The binary cartesian product operator ($\times$) retrieves all possible combinations of the tuples from the operand relations:

$$\mathsf{q} \times \mathsf{r} = \{t_q t_r | t_q \in \mathsf{q} \text{ and } t_r \in \mathsf{r}\}.$$

A simplifying assumption for the product operator is that the operand relations do not have any attribute names in common (i.e., $Q \cap R = \emptyset$). Otherwise, the relation resulting from the product would have duplicate attribute names.

As shown in Table 2.1, the schema of $\mathsf{q} \times \mathsf{r}$ represented as a set of attributes is $Q \cup R$. The degree of the resulting relation is the sum of the degree of the operand relations (i.e., degree(q) + degree(r)). The cardinality of $\mathsf{q} \times \mathsf{r}$, denoted $|\mathsf{q} \times \mathsf{r}|$, is the result of multiplying the cardinality of the operand relations (i.e., $|\mathsf{q}| * |\mathsf{r}|$).

Consider an example query over the EMPLOYEE TRAINING enterprise that retrieves all possible combinations of employees (eID) with training courses (cID):

$\surd Q_{\times}:\quad \pi_{\texttt{eID}}(\texttt{employee}) \times \pi_{\texttt{cID}}(\texttt{trainingCourse});$

This query may not appear quite useful. However, the cartesian product and selection operators provide the foundation for a *join* operator, which is one of the most used operations in relational databases. The join operator is discussed in the next section.

2.2 ADDITIONAL OPERATORS

The additional binary operators presented in this section are convenient shorthand notation for frequently used combinations of the fundamental operators. Table 2.2 provides a summary of the definition of the additional operators in terms of the fundamental operators.

TABLE 2.2 Summary of additional relational algebra operators.

Expression	Definition in Terms of Fundamental Operators
$r \cap s$	$r - (r - s)$
$p \bowtie_{\theta} q$	$\sigma_{\theta}(p \times q)$
$p \bowtie q$	$\pi_{P \cup Q}(\sigma_{p.ai=q.ai \text{ and } \ldots \text{ and } p.aj=q.aj}(p \times q))$, where $P \cap Q = \{ai, \ldots, aj\}$
$p \div q$	$\pi_{P-Q}(p) - \pi_{P-Q}((\pi_{P-Q}(p) \times q) - p)$

Intersection. The intersection operator ($\cap$) returns those tuples that are in both operand relations:

$$\mathsf{r} \cap \mathsf{s} = \{t \mid t \in \mathsf{r} \text{ and } t \in \mathsf{s}\}.$$

This is equivalent to the following relational algebra expression in terms of only the fundamental operators:

$$r \cap s = r - (r - s).$$

The operand relations of an intersection must be compatible. The resulting intersection has the same schema and degree of the operand relations. The cardinality of the intersection is the number of tuples that are in both relations.

Consider an example query over the EMPLOYEE TRAINING enterprise that retrieves the identification number of employees who are managers and have taken at least one training course:

$\surd Q_{\cap}$: $\pi_{\texttt{eID}}(\sigma_{\texttt{eTitle='Manager'}}(\texttt{employee})) \cap \pi_{\texttt{eID}}(\texttt{takes});$

Join. The join operator ($\bowtie_\theta$) is defined as a cartesian product of the operand relations followed by a selection using the θ condition:

$$\mathsf{p} \bowtie_\theta \mathsf{q} = \sigma_\theta(\mathsf{p} \times \mathsf{q})$$

Consider the following abstract schema and instance for relations p and q:

p

p1	p2
x1	y1
x2	y2

q

q1	q2
y1	z1
y2	z2
y1	z3
y3	z4

The resulting cartesian product of p and q has eight tuples:

p × q

p1	p2	q1	q2
x1	y1	y1	z1
x1	y1	y2	z2
x1	y1	y1	z3
x1	y1	y3	z4
x2	y2	y1	z1
x2	y2	y2	z2
x2	y2	y1	z3
x2	y2	y3	z4

Assuming that the join condition is p2 = q1, then the result of p $\bowtie_{p2=q1}$ q is

p $\bowtie_{p2=q1}$ q

p1	p2	q1	q2
x1	y1	y1	z1
x1	y1	y1	z3
x2	y2	y2	z2

As another example, consider the following query over the EMPLOYEE TRAINING enterprise that retrieves the employees who lead technology areas:

$\sqrt{Q_{\bowtie\theta}}$: employee $\bowtie_{eID=aLeadID}$ technologyArea;

This query represents the join of the employee and technologyArea tables such that the employee identification number is equal to the identification number of the area lead. The schema of the resulting join contains all the attributes of the employee and technologyArea tables. Thus, the degree of the join is nine. If only some of the attributes are desired, a projection operation can easily be introduced. The cardinality of the join is the same as the cardinality of technologyArea, since there is exactly one eID value that matches the value of the aLeadID foreign key attribute.

Natural Join. A natural join ($\bowtie$) is a shorthand notation for a join that occurs quite frequently in practice. The join condition is assumed to be a conjunction of equality atoms such that the value of attributes with the same name in both operand relations are equal. A projection is automatically introduced to include only one copy of the duplicate attributes, as in

$$p \bowtie q = \pi_{P \cup Q}(\sigma_{p.ai=q.ai \text{ and } \ldots \text{ and } p.aj=q.aj}(p \times q)),$$

where $P \cap Q = \{ai, \ldots, aj\}$.

Consider the following modified abstract schema and instance for relations p and q:

p

p1	p2q1
x1	y1
x2	y2

q

p2q1	q2
y1	z1
y2	z2
y3	z3

The natural join of p and q is

p $\bowtie$ q

p1	p2q1	q2
x1	y1	z1
x2	y2	z2

Consider an example query over the EMPLOYEE TRAINING enterprise that retrieves the course title and offerings of each training course:

$\surd Q_{\bowtie}$: $\pi_{\texttt{cTitle,tYear,tMonth,tDay}}$(trainingCourse ⋈ takes);

The natural join trainingCourse ⋈ takes joins the trainingCourse and takes tables such that the cID attributes in both tables are equal. The resulting schema for the natural join contains only one copy of the cID attribute, which is not projected in the result of the query.

Division. The division operator (÷) is one of the more complicated relational algebra operators. The types of queries that use the division operator typically find those values in the first operand relation that are related to *all* of the values in the second operand relation. Therefore, for the division operation p ÷ q to be a valid expression, $Q \subseteq P$. The schema of the division result p ÷ q is $P - Q$. A tuple t is in $p \div q$ if for all tuples $t_q \in$ q, there exists a tuple $t_p \in$ p such that $t_p.(Q) = t_q$ and $t_p.(P - Q) = t$. This division operation looks quite complicated in terms of the fundamental relational algebra operators:

$$p \div q = \pi_{P-Q}(p) - \pi_{P-Q}((\pi_{P-Q}(p) \times q) - p).$$

The details of this equivalence are addressed in the next section, which introduces notation that allows us to break down a large query into a sequence of intermediate relations.

First, consider the following example to motivate the division operator on an abstract example abTable ÷ bTable, where the schemas of the operand relations are abTable(a,b) and bTable(b):

abTable

a	b
a1	b1
a1	b2
a2	b2
a3	b1
a3	b2
a3	b3

bTable

b
b1
b2

Suppose that the query is to find the a's from the abTable that are related to *all* of the b's specified in the bTable. The answer is given by abTable ÷ bTable:

abTable ÷ bTable

a
a1
a3

The value a2 is not in the result, since a2 is not related to both b1 and b2.

A detailed division example based on the Employee Training enterprise will be presented later in the chapter. The next section introduces notation that allows us to break down a large query, such as the definition of division in terms of the fundamental relational algebra operators, into a sequence of intermediate relations.

2.3 INTERMEDIATE RELATIONS AND RENAMING

There is no need to specify a query as a single relational algebra expression. Often, it makes sense to break down a query into smaller understandable parts, saving each part as an intermediate relation with a self-describing name.

The example query $Q_{\cap}$ over the Employee Training enterprise can be broken down into smaller parts with named intermediate relations. First, define the managers relation as the identification number of employees with the title 'Manager':

√ $\texttt{managers} := \pi_{\texttt{eID}}(\sigma_{\texttt{eTitle='Manager'}}(\texttt{employee}));$

Then, define an intermediate relation takenCourse that has the identification number of employees that have taken a training course:

√ $\texttt{takenCourse} := \pi_{\texttt{eID}}(\texttt{takes});$

The answer to the query is the intersection of these two intermediate relations:

√ $\texttt{managers} \cap \texttt{takenCourse};$

The assignment of a query expression to an intermediate relation also allows for the renaming of attributes, which is useful for setting up the schemas of the intermediate relations for compatibility with specific relational algebra operators.

Consider an example query over the Employee Training enterprise that retrieves the identification number of employees who are managers or lead a technology area. The managers intermediate relation is already defined from the previous example. The identification numbers of employees who lead a technology area is accessed by a projection on the aLeadID attribute of the technologyArea table:

√ $\texttt{leads(eID)} := \pi_{\texttt{aLeadID}}(\texttt{technologyArea});$

Note that the aLeadID attribute is renamed to eID in the definition of leads so that the managers and leads intermediate relations are compatible for answering the query using a union:

√ $\texttt{managers} \cup \texttt{leads};$

Division Revisited

A detailed explanation of the division operator in terms of the fundamental relational algebra operators is an appropriate example for breaking down a query into smaller parts. Consider the definition of division as expressed using only the fundamental relational algebra operators in the context of the abstract example:

√ $\pi_{\texttt{a}}(\texttt{abTable}) - \pi_{\texttt{a}}((\pi_{\texttt{a}}(\texttt{abTable}) \times \texttt{bTable}) - \texttt{abTable});$

Let's break down this division definition into more manageable parts. The first part defines a table containing the a's that appear in the `abTable`:

√ $\texttt{aTable} := \pi_{\texttt{a}}(\texttt{abTable});$

The second part specifies all possible combinations of a's with b's:

√ $\texttt{allaWithAllb} := \texttt{aTable} \times \texttt{bTable};$

The third part finds the a's that are not related to some b by taking all possibilities and subtracting the actual relationships given by the `abTable` and then projecting on attribute a:

√ $\texttt{aNotRelatedToSomeb} := \pi_{\texttt{a}}(\texttt{allaWithAllb} - \texttt{abTable});$

The last part returns the a's related to *all* b's by taking all possible a's and subtracting those a's that are not related to some b:

√ `aRelatedToAllb := aTable − aNotRelatedToSomeb;`

For those familiar with the logical equivalences of universal and existential quantification, this formulation of division should be somewhat intuitive. These logical equivalences will be discussed in the relational calculus chapters.

2.4 EXAMPLE QUERIES

Earlier in this chapter, simple queries introduced the various relational algebra operators. In this section, nontrivial queries over the EMPLOYEE TRAINING enterprise illustrate various types of database queries, including negation and division. Although relational algebra does not inherently support aggregation, these examples also include creative solutions for queries involving a limited form of counting and finding a minimum value. Each query specification includes an English description and a listing of the attributes to appear in the result schema.

Query Q1 illustrates a typical query over the EMPLOYEE TRAINING enterprise, finding the training courses offered in a particular technology area, such as the database area. The intermediate table dbTechArea contains a single tuple having the unique identification number for the database technology area. This simple relation is then natural joined with trainingCourse to select those training courses in the database technology area.

√Q1: What training courses are offered in the 'Database' technology area?

(cID, cTitle, cHours)

dbTechArea(areaID) := $\pi_{\texttt{aID}}(\sigma_{\texttt{aTitle='Database'}}(\texttt{technologyArea}))$;
q1 := $\pi_{\texttt{cID,cTitle,cHours}}(\texttt{dbTechArea} \bowtie \texttt{trainingCourse})$;

Query Q2 finds those employees who have taken training courses in the database technology area. Using the result of Q1, the intermediate table dbCourseID contains the unique identification number of the courses offered in the database technology area. The dbCourseID table is then joined with the takes table to find the IDs of employees who have taken a database course, which is then joined with employee to retrieve the requested attributes for the query result.

√Q2: Which employees have taken a training course offered in the 'Database' technology area?

(eID, eLast, eFirst, eTitle)

dbCourseID := $\pi_{\texttt{cID}}(\texttt{q1})$;
q2 := $\pi_{\texttt{eID,eLast,eFirst,eTitle}}((\texttt{dbCourseID} \bowtie \texttt{takes}) \bowtie \texttt{employee})$;

Query Q3 illustrates a database query that involves negation, finding those employees who have not taken any training courses. The alleIDs intermediate table contains the eID value for all employees. The takeseIDs intermediate table contains the eID value for those employees that have taken at least one course. The employees who have not taken any training courses is obtained by subtracting takeseIDs from alleIDs. The difference is then joined with the employee table to return the specified attributes.

√Q3: Which employees have not taken any training courses?

(eID, eLast, eFirst, eTitle)

alleIDs := $\pi_{\texttt{eID}}(\texttt{employee})$;

takeseIDs := $\pi_{\texttt{eID}}$(takes);
q3 := $\pi_{\texttt{eID,eLast,eFirst,eTitle}}$((alleIDs − takeseIDs) ⋈ employee);

Query Q4 illustrates how one can use the relational algebra operators to support a limited form of counting by finding those employees who took courses in *more than one* technology area. The intermediate table `eIDaIDs` contains the identifiers of employees along with the area identifier of the training courses that the employees have taken. The intermediate table `eIDaIDsCopy` is a copy of the `eIDaIDs` table with the attributes renamed. By joining `eIDaIDs` with its copy such that the employee identifiers are the same and the area identifiers are different gives the employees who have taken courses in more than one technology area. The intermediate table `eIDsMoreThanOne` is natural joined with `employee` to return the desired attributes.

√Q4: Which employees took courses in more than one technology area?

(eID, eLast, eFirst, eTitle)

eIDaIDs(eID, aID) := $\pi_{\texttt{eID,areaID}}$(takes ⋈ trainingCourse);
eIDaIDsCopy(eID1, aID1) := eIDaIDs;
eIDsMoreThanOne := $\pi_{\texttt{eID}}$(eIDaIDs $\bowtie_{\texttt{eID=eID1 and aID<>aID1}}$ eIDaIDsCopy);
q4 := $\pi_{\texttt{eID,eLast,eFirst,eTitle}}$(eIDsMoreThanOne ⋈ employee);

Query Q5 shows how to write a query to find the employees who have the minimum salary. The intermediate tables `empSal` and `empSalCopy` each contain a single attribute consisting of employee salaries, but have different attribute names. The intermediate table `empSalNotMin` finds those employee salaries that are *not* minimum by joining the employee salary tables and selecting those salaries that are greater than another salary. The minimum salary is obtained by subtracting the salaries that are not minimum from all employee salaries. The intermediate table `empSalMin` is joined with `employee` to find the employee(s) having the minimum salary.

√Q5: Which employees have the minimum salary?

(eID, eLast, eFirst, eTitle, eSalary)

empSal := $\pi_{\texttt{eSalary}}$(employee);
empSalCopy(eSalary1) := empSal;
empSalNotMin := $\pi_{\texttt{eSalary}}$(empSal $\bowtie_{\texttt{eSalary>eSalary1}}$ empSalCopy);
empSalMin := empSal - empSalNotMin;
q5 := employee ⋈ empSalMin;

Query Q6 illustrates a database query that involves division, finding those employees who took *all* of the training courses offered in the database technology area. Since the schema of dbCourseID (from Q2) consists of the single attribute cID, the schema of the intermediate table empsAllDB consists of the single attribute eID, which contains the IDs of employees who took all of the database courses. The table empsAllDB is then joined with employee to retrieve the desired attributes for the result.

√Q6: Which employees took all of the training courses offered in the 'Database' technology area?

(eID, eLast, eFirst, eTitle)

$\text{empsAllDB} := \pi_{\text{eID},\text{cID}}(\text{takes}) \div \text{dbCourseID};$
$\text{q6} := \pi_{\text{eID},\text{eLast},\text{eFirst},\text{eTitle}}(\text{empsAllDB} \bowtie \text{employee});$

2.5 QUERY OPTIMIZATION

There are multiple ways to write a relational algebra expression to correctly answer a query. Recall the query Q1 from the example queries that finds the training courses offered in the database technology area. Consider combining the two steps into one relational algebra expression:

√ $\pi_{\text{cID},\text{cTitle},\text{cHours}}(\pi_{\text{aID}}(\sigma_{\text{aTitle}='\text{Database}'}(\text{technologyArea})) \bowtie_{\text{aID}=\text{areaID}} \text{trainingCourse});$

The following relational algebra expression finds the same set of tuples:

√ $\pi_{\text{cID},\text{cTitle},\text{cHours}}(\sigma_{\text{aTitle}='\text{Database}'}(\text{technologyArea} \bowtie_{\text{aID}=\text{areaID}} \text{trainingCourse}));$

The first specification of the query finds the database technology area, which is then joined with the trainingCourse table to answer the query. The second specification joins the entire technologyArea and trainingCourse tables and then selects the tuples corresponding to the database technology area. In general, the first specification should be more efficient to evaluate than the second since a smaller number of tuples are involved in the join.

Consider as another example the query Q2 combined into a single relational algebra expression that finds the employees who have taken a training course offered in the database technology area:

√ $\pi_{\text{eID},\text{eLast},\text{eFirst},\text{eTitle}}((\text{q1} \bowtie \text{takes}) \bowtie \text{employee});$

The following relational algebra expression finds the same set of tuples:

√ $\pi_{\texttt{eID,eLast,eFirst,eTitle}}(\texttt{q1} \bowtie (\texttt{takes} \bowtie \texttt{employee}))$;

The first formulation of the query joins the database course IDs (given by `q1`) with the `takes` table to find the employees that took a database course. The second formulation of the query joins `takes` and `employee` first, finding the employee information associated with *every* takes tuple in the database. Next, the database training courses in `q1` are joined with the result of joining `takes` and `employee`. In general, the first specification should be more efficient to evaluate than the second, since the order of the joins in the first query results in intermediate expressions that have a smaller number of tuples.

An exhaustive search of the alternatives for evaluating a query can cost more than the evaluation of the query as given. Therefore, a heuristic approach is generally taken to minimize the number of tuples in the intermediate expressions within the query. The motivational examples illustrated (1) the *performing selections as early as possible* optimization using Q1, and (2) the *reordering of joins* optimization using Q2. These optimizations are based on the theoretical properties of the relational algebra operators. For example, the natural join operator is both commutative and associative.

The automation of query optimization is complex and requires knowledge of the various statistics on the tables in the database, including the following:

- the number of tuples in each table
- the number of unique values of each attribute in the table
- the physical storage characteristics of the table and associated index structures

These statistics are costly to maintain for each insertion, deletion, or modification to the database. Typically, these statistics are gathered using a separate utility program that the database administrator schedules to run periodically when the database is not heavily utilized.

2.6 SUMMARY

This chapter covered the relational algebra query language, which is a formal and procedural query language. The fundamental operators ($\sigma, \pi, \cup, -, \times$) that characterize the required operations for effectively retrieving data from a relational database were introduced using detailed examples. Examples were also given to motivate the additional relational operators ($\cap, \bowtie_{\theta}, \bowtie, \div$) that are convenient shorthand notation for frequently used combinations of the fundamental operators. Additional example queries over the EMPLOYEE TRAINING enterprise illustrated the use of relational algebra on various types of database queries. The chapter concluded with a brief discussion on query optimization, which provided motivational examples to illustrate several approaches to answering the same query using relational algebra.

EXERCISES

√ Use the WinRDBI educational tool to *check* the answers to these marked exercises.

√**2.1** Answer the following queries in relational algebra over the EMPLOYEE TRAINING schema:

```
employee(eID, eLast, eFirst, eTitle, eSalary)
technologyArea(aID, aTitle, aURL, aLeadID)
trainingCourse(cID, cTitle, cHours, areaID)
takes(eID, cID, tYear, tMonth, tDay)
```

(a) What are the titles of employees who lead technology areas?

`(eTitle)`

(b) Which employees have not taken any training courses in the 'Database' technology area?

`(eID, eLast, eFirst, eTitle)`

(c) Which employees took courses in *only one* technology area?

`(eID, eLast, eFirst, eTitle)`

(*Hint*: This type of query is not inherently supported by relational algebra. However, this can be expressed in relational algebra by finding those employees who took a course in one technology area and did not take courses in more than one technology area.)

(d) What is the maximum salary of employees who lead technology areas?

`(eSalary)`

(e) Which employees have taken at least one training course in *all* of the technology areas offered by the company?

`(eID, eLast, eFirst, eTitle)`

√**2.2** Data validation is an important feature of database systems. Chapter 1 discussed various constraints, such as the primary key constraint and referential integrity. In relational database products, these constraints are specified in the definition of the database schema and inherently supported by the database system during operation. However, there are possible scenarios that can occur when you may need to verify these constraints outside of a database system, such as data residing in a text file.

Another scenario is data represented as a collection of facts in a Prolog program, which is the approach used in the WinRDBI educational tool. Therefore, the tool does not inherently support these constraints. Write queries in relational algebra to find violations of the following constraints over the EMPLOYEE TRAINING schema. Hopefully, you won't find any violations in the database instance given. You should make a copy of the EMPLOYEE TRAINING database and introduce errors to verify the specification of your queries. (You may assume that there are no null values.)

(a) Primary Key Constraint
Choose one of the tables from the EMPLOYEE TRAINING database schema, and write a relational algebra query to find violations of the primary key constraint; that is, find key values that appear more than once in the table.

(b) Referential Integrity Constraint
Choose one of the referential integrity constraints in the EMPLOYEE TRAINING database schema, and write a relational algebra query to find violations of the referential integrity constraint; that is, find foreign key values that do not have a corresponding value as a primary key.

(c) Cardinality Ratio
Write a relational algebra query to find violations of the constraint requiring that an employee can lead at most one technology area.

√**2.3** Query optimization is another important feature of database systems. Examine your answers to Exercises 2.1 and 2.2. Can your relational algebra expressions be optimized by performing selections earlier or by modifying the join ordering? Verify your solutions on the educational tool.

Postscript

You will get a chance to answer additional relational algebra queries over the EMPLOYEE TRAINING *example. New queries are given in each of the chapters on DRC, TRC and SQL. However, you are encouraged to work out those queries in relational algebra after you have answered them first in the query language specified in the chapter. Why? Some people have the tendency to translate the queries from one language to another, rather than taking advantage of the inherent features of the query language being studied.*

Chapter 3

Domain Relational Calculus

Relational calculus is a declarative query language and indicates the properties of the data to be retrieved instead of the procedural paradigm of relational algebra that specifies the operations required to retrieve the data. There are two types of relational calculus query languages: domain and tuple. In DRC, the variables range over the domain of an attribute. In TRC, the variables range over tuples of a relation. This chapter covers the DRC language, which is strongly related to the use of declarative languages for the integration of database and artificial intelligence technologies. The next chapter describes the TRC language, which is essentially the foundation of the basic query expression in SQL.

Although the declarative expressions of the DRC language differ from the procedural operators of relational algebra, the DRC language is *relationally complete*. A query expressible in relational algebra can be expressed in DRC. The relational completeness of DRC is illustrated by example, expressing the examples using the fundamental and additional operators of relational algebra in DRC. DRC solutions for the six sample queries over the EMPLOYEE TRAINING enterprise further illustrate the differences between DRC's declarative approach and relational algebra's imperative approach.

3.1 EXPRESSIONS

There are many accepted variations on the syntax for DRC expressions. The syntax introduced here is consistent with this book's notation that assumes relation (and attribute) names are identifiers starting with a lowercase letter. Identifiers that begin with an uppercase letter denote variables, and constants are either single-quoted strings or numeric constants. Instead of using the mathematical symbols denoting negation ($\neg$), conjunction ($\wedge$), disjunction ($\vee$), existential quantification ($\exists$), and universal quantification ($\forall$), the words `not`, `and`, `or`, `exists`, and `forall`, respectively, are used.

A general DRC expression is of the form

$$\{D1, D2, \ldots, Dn \mid \mathcal{F}(D1, D2, \ldots, Dn)\},$$

where $\mathcal{F}$ is a DRC formula describing the properties that are to hold true on the data to be retrieved. The output schema of $\mathcal{F}$ is given by the domain variables D1, D2, ..., Dn. The result of the DRC expression is the set of all tuples (d1, d2, ..., dn) such that when di is substituted for Di ($1 \leq i \leq n$), the formula $\mathcal{F}$ is true.

The building block of a DRC formula is an atom and consists of a reference to a relation or a comparison of a domain variable to another domain variable or domain constant. An atom forms the basis of a formula, which is built up from atoms using logical connectives (`not, and, or`) and quantification (`exists, forall`).

Let

`r` be a relation of degree n
Di be a domain variable
c be a domain constant
θ be a comparison operator (<, =<, =, >, >=, <>), and assume that its operands are comparable by θ.

An atom is of the form

- `r(D1, D2, ..., Dn)`
  TRUE when D1, D2, ..., Dn are assigned values forming a tuple in `r`.
- `Di` θ `Dj`
  TRUE when Di θ Dj is TRUE; otherwise, it is FALSE.
- `Di` θ `c`
  TRUE when Di θ c is TRUE; otherwise, it is FALSE.

A formula is composed of atoms using the following rules:

(1) An atom is a formula.
Its meaning is given by the truth value of the atom.

(2) Let $\mathcal{F}$, $\mathcal{F}1$, and $\mathcal{F}2$ be formulas, then the following are formulas:

- ($\mathcal{F}$)
  TRUE when $\mathcal{F}$ is TRUE and otherwise FALSE.

- not $\mathcal{F}$
  TRUE when $\mathcal{F}$ is FALSE and otherwise FALSE.
- $\mathcal{F}1$ and $\mathcal{F}2$
  TRUE when both $\mathcal{F}1$ and $\mathcal{F}2$ are TRUE and otherwise FALSE.
- $\mathcal{F}1$ or $\mathcal{F}2$
  TRUE when either $\mathcal{F}1$ or $\mathcal{F}2$ are TRUE and otherwise FALSE.

(3) Let $\mathcal{F}$(D) be a formula in which the variable D appears free. A variable is free if it is not quantified by an existential or universal quantifier. Then the following are formulas:

- (exists D)$\mathcal{F}$(D)
  TRUE if there exists a value assigned to D that makes $\mathcal{F}$(D) TRUE and otherwise FALSE.
- (forall D)$\mathcal{F}$(D)
  TRUE if any value that is assigned to D makes $\mathcal{F}$(D) TRUE and otherwise FALSE.

A valid DRC expression {D1, D2, . . . , Dn | $\mathcal{F}$(D1, D2, . . . , Dn)} has only the domain variables D1, D2, . . ., Dn free in $\mathcal{F}$. A free variable in a DRC expression is analogous to a global variable in a programming language. Any other variable appearing in $\mathcal{F}$ must be a bound variable, which is similar to a local variable, and is declared through quantification. The scope of the bound variable is the quantified formula. The most commonly used quantifier is `exists`, although the `forall` quantifier is used for division type queries. The DRC language is illustrated by example in the remainder of the chapter.

Intermediate relations were introduced in the previous chapter to materialize the result of a relational algebra expression. The concept of intermediate tables is not restricted to the relational algebra language, but applies to a query expression in any relational query language. Thus, the syntax

```
intermediateTable := queryExpression;
```

assigns the result of the `queryExpression` to the `intermediateTable`.

3.2 EXPRESSIVE POWER

The DRC language is *relationally complete*, which means that any query expressible in relational algebra is expressible in DRC. Examples over the EMPLOYEE TRAINING enterprise illustrate both the expressive power of DRC and the features of the language. In the examples, the names of the domain variables are based on the identifier of the variable's associated attribute. In most cases, the initial letter of the attribute name is capitalized to form the identifier of the domain variable. Although abbreviated domain variable names are possible, this naming convention results in self-documenting examples.

3.2.1 Fundamental Operators

The fundamental relational algebra operators characterize the required operations for effectively retrieving information from a relational database. Table 3.1 summarizes the DRC expressions for operations involving the fundamental relational algebra operators.

Table 3.2 provides the DRC queries that correspond to the illustrative examples over the EMPLOYEE TRAINING enterprise using the fundamental operators.

Query Q_σ:

```
√ { EID, ELast, EFirst, ETitle, ESalary |
      employee(EID, ELast, EFirst, ETitle, ESalary) and
      ESalary > 100000 };
```

TABLE 3.1 DRC summary of fundamental relational algebra operators.

Algebra	DRC
σ_θ(r)	{R1, ... Rn | r(R1, ..., Rn) and θ }
π_A(r)	{ Ri, ... Rj | r(R1, ..., Ri, ..., Rj, ..., Rn) }
r ∪ s	{ D1, ... Dn | r(D1, ..., Dn) or s(D1, ..., Dn) }
r − s	{ D1, ... Dn | r(D1, ..., Dn) and not s(D1, ..., Dn) }
q × r	{ Q1, ... Qm, R1, ... Rn | q(Q1, ..., Qm) and r(R1, ..., Rn) }

TABLE 3.2 DRC summary of fundamental EMPLOYEE TRAINING queries.

Query	√DRC
Q_σ	{ EID, ELast, EFirst, ETitle, ESalary | employee(EID, ELast, EFirst, ETitle, ESalary) and ESalary > 100000 };
Q_π	{ ELast, EFirst, ETitle | employee(_, ELast, EFirst, ETitle, _) };
$Q_\cup$	managers := { EID | employee(EID, _, _, 'Manager', _) }; coaches := { EID | employee(EID, _, _, 'Coach', _) }; { EID | managers(EID) or coaches(EID) };
Q_-	managers := { EID | employee(EID, _, _, 'Manager', _) }; takenCourse := { EID | takes(EID, _, _, _, _) }; { EID | managers(EID) and not takenCourse(EID) };
$Q_\times$	{ EID, CID | employee(EID, _, _, _, _) and trainingCourse(CID, _, _, _) };

The domain variables (EID, ELast, EFirst, ETitle, ESalary) forming the output schema of the DRC expression are the only variables that appear in the DRC formula. These variables are free variables, since they are not quantified within the DRC formula. The atom employee(EID, ELast, EFirst, ETitle, ESalary) binds the variables to values, forming a tuple in the employee relation. The atom ESalary > 100000 then checks whether the employee's salary is greater than 100,000.

Query Q_π:

The query Q_π in Table 3.2 is derived from shortcuts that the DRC language allows. The resulting query is derived from the following sequence of queries. Initially, the first attempt at this query, according to the definition of a DRC expression, introduces the free or global variables for the result of the projection (ELast, EFirst, ETitle) and declares the local domain variables EID and ESalary to hold the position of those attributes in the reference to the employee table. The local variables are bound by the existential quantifiers can be specified in the scope of the quantified formula:

```
√ { ELast, EFirst, ETitle | (exists EID)(exists ESalary)
      (employee(EID, ELast, EFirst, ETitle, ESalary)) };
```

There is a shortcut syntax available for quantifying multiple variables in the DRC language. Rather than specifying the existential quantifier for each domain variable, the existential quantifier can be specified once for a list of variables:

```
√ { ELast, EFirst, ETitle | (exists EID, ESalary)
      (employee(EID, ELast, EFirst, ETitle, ESalary)) };
```

The values of the bound variables EID and ESalary are not explicitly referenced by the query, but are required based on the *by-position* syntax of the DRC language, referencing an attribute by its position in the tuple of a relation. To avoid the verbosity of quantifying and using a domain variable for every attribute of every relation in a query specification, an *anonymous* variable, denoted by _, can be used when the value of an attribute is not referenced. In this query, the attributes eID and eSalary of the employee relation are not of interest. Therefore, anonymous variables (_) can hold the positions of those attributes in the relation reference.

```
√ { ELast, EFirst, ETitle |
      employee(_, ELast, EFirst, ETitle, _) };
```

Query $Q_\cup$:

The query $Q_\cup$ displayed in Table 3.2 illustrates another shortcut allowed by the DRC language.

Consider an initial specification of the union query that defines an intermediate table for managers and coaches. In each intermediate table definition, a local variable ETitle is introduced to test the value of the eTitle attribute. The third expression unions the compatible intermediate tables managers and coaches. The domain variable EID is free in the union DRC expression, getting its bindings from the operands of the disjunction. Therefore, the disjuncts of a valid disjunctive expression must have the same free variables:

```
√ managers := { EID | (exists ETitle)
      (employee(EID, _, _, ETitle, _) and ETitle='Manager') };
  coaches := { EID | (exists ETitle)
      (employee(EID, _, _, ETitle, _) and ETitle='Coach') };
  { EID | managers(EID) or coaches(EID) };
```

In this example, the bound variable ETitle is introduced to check that its value is equal to 'Manager' in the definition of managers and 'Coach' in the definition of coaches, respectively. If a domain variable is only referenced in an equality check with a domain constant, then that domain constant can be used directly in the relation reference. In this example, the domain constants 'Manager' and 'Coach' can be used directly, thereby eliminating the need for the domain variable ETitle:

```
√ managers := { EID | employee(EID, _, _, 'Manager', _) };
  coaches := { EID | employee(EID, _, _, 'Coach', _) };
  { EID | managers(EID) or coaches(EID) };
```

The previous versions of this query purposely follow the general template for expressing a union in DRC. However, this query can also be phrased as the single query:

```
√ { EID | (exists ETitle) (employee(EID, _, _, ETitle, _) and
    (ETitle = 'Manager' or ETitle = 'Coach') ) };
```

Query Q_-:

```
√ managers := { EID | employee(EID, _, _, 'Manager', _) };
  takenCourse := { EID | takes(EID, _, _, _, _) };
  { EID | managers(EID) and not takenCourse(EID) };
```

The query Q_- purposely follows a general template for expressing a difference in DRC. It is not necessary to create the managers and takenCourse intermediate tables. The query can be specified in one step:

```
√ { EID | employee(EID, _, _, 'Manager', _) and
     not takes(EID, _, _, _, _) };
```

Query $Q_\times$:

```
√ { EID, CID | employee(EID, _, _, _, _) and
      trainingCourse(CID, _, _, _) };
```

Recall that the simplifying assumption for the product operator of relational algebra requires that the operand relations of the product do not have any attribute names in common. The use of different domain variable names in DRC achieves the analogy of this simplifying assumption. Since the output schema consists of only the `EID` and `CID` domain variables, anonymous variables are used to construct the needed relation references.

3.2.2 Additional Operators

The additional binary operators ($\cap$, $\bowtie_\theta$, $\bowtie$, $\div$) are convenient shorthand notation for frequently used combinations of the fundamental operators of relational algebra. The illustrative examples over the EMPLOYEE TRAINING enterprise using the additional operators ($\cap$, $\bowtie_\theta$, $\bowtie$) are summarized in Table 3.3. The division operator ($\div$) is not shown in the table, since a more detailed discussion of this complex operator is justified and appears later in this section.

TABLE 3.3 DRC summary of additional EMPLOYEE TRAINING queries.

Query	√DRC

$Q_\cap$	`managers := { EID | employee(EID, _, _, 'Manager', _) };`
	`takenCourse := { EID | takes(EID, _, _, _,_) };`
	`{ EID | managers(EID) and takenCourse(EID) };`

$Q_{\bowtie_\theta}$	`{ EID, ELast, EFirst, ETitle, ESalary, AID, ATitle, AURL, ALeadID |`
	`employee(EID, ELast, EFirst, ETitle, ESalary) and`
	`technologyArea(AID, ATitle, AURL, ALeadID) and EID=ALeadID };`

$Q_\bowtie$	`{ CTitle, TYear, TMonth, TDay | (exists CID)`
	`(trainingCourse(CID, CTitle, _, _) and`
	`takes(_, CID, TYear, TMonth, TDay)) };`

Query $Q_\cap$:

```
√ managers := { EID | employee(EID, _, _, 'Manager', _) };
  takenCourse := { EID | takes(EID, _, _, _,_) };
  { EID | managers(EID) and takenCourse(EID) };
```

The use of the same domain variable name (`EID`) in both atoms referencing the intermediate tables (`managers` and `takenCourse`) results in the intersection of these operand relations.

Similar to the queries $Q_{\cup}$ and Q_{-}, query $Q_{\cap}$ follows a general template for expressing its corresponding operation in DRC by introducing intermediate tables on which to perform the intersection. Again, the introduction of the intermediate tables is unnecessary, and the query can be answered in one step:

```
√ { EID | employee(EID, _, _, 'Manager', _) and
      takes(EID, _, _, _, _) };
```

$Q_{\bowtie_\theta}$:

```
√  { EID, ELast, EFirst, ETitle, ESalary,
       AID, ATitle, AURL, ALeadID |
       employee(EID, ELast, EFirst, ETitle, ESalary) and
       technologyArea(AID, ATitle, AURL, ALeadID) and
       EID=ALeadID };
```

The query $Q_{\bowtie_\theta}$ represents a join of the `employee` and `technologyArea` tables such that the `aLeadID` attribute of `technologyArea` is equal to the `eID` attribute of `employee`. To be consistent with the original relational algebra specification of this query, all of the attributes of both operand tables are included in the query result:

$Q_{\bowtie}$:

```
√  { CTitle, TYear, TMonth, TDay | (exists CID)
       (trainingCourse(CID, CTitle, _, _) and
       takes(_, CID, TYear, TMonth, TDay)) };
```

In DRC, using the same domain variable name in the positions that are to be joined results in a natural join. Since the output schema does not include the `cID` attribute that is to be natural joined, the domain variable `CID` must be declared locally and bound in the formula. In this situation, the existential quantifier is used, indicating that there exists a value for the `CID` variable in both tables that makes the formula true.

Division. The division operator ($\div$) is one of the more complicated relational algebra operators. The types of queries that use the division operator typically find those values in the first operand relation that are related to *all* of the values in the second operand relation.

Recall the following abstract example to illustrate the division operation `abTable` $\div$ `bTable`, where the schemas of the operand relations are `abTable(a,b)` and `bTable(b)`:

abTable

a	b
a1	b1
a1	b2
a2	b2
a3	b1
a3	b2
a3	b3

bTable

b
b1
b2

Remember that the query is to find the a's from the abTable that are related to *all* of the b's specified in the bTable. The answer is given by abTable ÷ bTable, consisting of the single attribute a and the tuples { (a1), (a3) }. The value a2 is not in the result, since a2 is not related to both b1 and b2.

In DRC, the abstract division example can be stated as follows: an A value is included in the result of the division, provided that the A value is in the abTable and for all possible B values, if B is in the bTable then the A and B values are related by the abTable.

```
{ A | abTable(A, _) and
      (forall B) (bTable(B) implies abTable(A,B) ) };
```

The implies operator has not been formally defined in this variation of the DRC language. However, p implies q is logically equivalent to not p or q. Therefore, the division example restated is

```
√ { A | abTable(A, _) and
      (forall B) (not bTable(B) or abTable(A,B) ) };
```

Table 3.4 shows the corresponding truth table. The forall formula must be true for all values of the variable B, including those B values that are not in the bTable.

There is another logically equivalent specification of division that uses only existential quantification. An A value is included in the result of the division, provided that the A value is in the abTable and it is not the case that there exists a B value that is in the bTable and is *not* related to the A value by the abTable:

```
√ { A | abTable(A, _) and not (exists B)
      (bTable(B) and not abTable(A,B)) };
```

This logically equivalent existential specification can be derived from the universal specification using the following logical equivalences:

- Given the universal specification

  ```
  √ { A | abTable(A, _) and
        (forall B) (not bTable(B) or abTable(A,B) ) };
  ```

TABLE 3.4 DRC division: universal truth table.

A	B	bTable(B)	abTable(A,B)	not bTable(B)	not bTable(B) or abTable(A,B)	forall B
a1	b1	T	T	F	T	
	b2	T	T	F	T	T
	b3	F	F	T	T	
a2	b1	T	F	F	F	
	b2	T	T	F	T	F
	b3	F	F	T	T	
a3	b1	T	T	F	T	
	b2	T	T	F	T	T
	b3	F	T	T	T	

TABLE 3.5 DRC division: existential truth table.

A	B	bTable(B)	not abTable(A,B)	bTable(B) and not abTable(A,B)	exists B	not exists B
a1	b1	T	F	F		
	b2	T	F	F	F	T
	b3	F	T	F		
a2	b1	T	T	T		
	b2	T	F	F	T	F
	b3	F	T	F		
a3	b1	T	F	F		
	b2	T	F	F	F	T
	b3	F	F	F		

- Apply the logical equivalence:
  `(forall D)` $\mathcal{F}$`(D)` ≡ `not (exists D) not` $\mathcal{F}$`(D)`

  √
```
{ A | abTable(A, _) and not (exists B) not
      (not bTable(B) or abTable(A,B) ) };
```

- Apply DeMorgan's Law: `not (p or q)` ≡ `not p and not q`

  √
```
{ A | abTable(A, _) and not (exists B)
      (bTable(B) and not abTable(A,B)) };
```

Table 3.5 shows the truth table for the resulting existential specification of the division abstract example.

3.2.3 Safety

The previous examples have demonstrated the relational completeness of DRC (i.e., how the operators of relational algebra can be expressed in DRC). Since the operand relations are finite and the relational algebra operators produce finite relations, the result of a relational algebra expression is finite. However, not all DRC expressions are finite. Consider the DRC expression that attempts to find employees that do not lead a technology area:

```
{ EID | not technologyArea(_, _, _, EID) }
```

There are infinitely many values that are not in the `aLeadID` attribute position of the `technologyArea` table. The appropriate query specification is to limit the `EID` variable to values of the `eID` attribute of the `employee` table and then check whether that value appears in the position of the `aLeadID` attribute in the `technologyArea` table:

```
√ { EID | employee(EID, _, _, _, _) and
      not technologyArea(_, _, _, EID) };
```

A *safe* DRC expression is one that guarantees a finite result. Intuitively, a safe DRC expression limits the values of a domain variable D (either directly or indirectly) by its appearance in a positive atom of the form `r( ... D ... )` or by constraining its values to be equal to that of a domain constant (e.g., `D = 'Manager'`). The examples illustrating the relational completeness of the DRC language are safe. Although it is not proven here, only *safe* DRC expressions can be realized in relational algebra. Therefore, relational algebra and safe DRC are equivalent in expressive power.

3.3 EXAMPLE QUERIES

The same nontrivial queries over the Employee Training enterprise are used to illustrate various types of database queries using the safe DRC language. By convention, the value of a domain variable is limited before its value is referenced in a left-to-right reading of the expression. Although this convention is not theoretically required, such a convention increases the readability of the examples.

As is the case with relational algebra, DRC does not inherently support aggregation capabilities, such as counting or finding minimum or maximum, which appear to be necessary to answer queries Q4 and Q5. However, there are creative solutions to these queries in DRC. To find those employees who took courses in more than one technology area, Query Q4 finds the employees such that there exists two `takes` tuples for that employee where the courses are from two different technology areas. Query Q5 finds the employees having the minimum salary by finding those employees such that it is not the case that there exists another employee having a smaller salary. The division query Q6 finds the employees who have taken all the training courses offered in the database technology area by finding employees who took at least one database course and it is not the case that there exists a database course that the employee has not taken. The intermediate table `dbEmployee` created in Query Q2 is reused in query Q6 to verify that the employee has taken at least one course. If this verification is not performed, incorrect results would be produced when the `dbCourse` intermediate table is empty.

√Q1: What training courses are offered in the database technology area?

```
(cID, cTitle, cHours)

dbCourse :=
    { CID, CTitle, CHours | (exists AID)
        (technologyArea(AID, 'Database', _, _) and
        trainingCourse(CID, CTitle, CHours, AID)) };
```

√Q2: Which employees have taken a training course offered in the database technology area?

```
(eID, eLast, eFirst, eTitle)

dbEmployee :=
    { EID, ELast, EFirst, ETitle | (exists CID)
        (dbCourse(CID, _, _) and takes(EID, CID, _, _, _) and
        employee(EID, ELast, EFirst, ETitle, _) ) };
```

√Q3: Which employees have not taken any training courses?

```
(eID, eLast, eFirst, eTitle)

{ EID, ELast, EFirst, ETitle |
    employee(EID, ELast, EFirst, ETitle, _) and
    not takes(EID, _, _, _, _) };
```

√Q4: Which employees took courses in more than one technology area?

```
(eID, eLast, eFirst, eTitle)

{ EID, ELast, EFirst, ETitle |
```

```
        employee(EID, ELast, EFirst, ETitle, _) and
        (exists CID1, CID2, AID1, AID2)
            (takes(EID, CID1, _, _, _) and
            trainingCourse(CID1, _, _, AID1) and
            takes(EID, CID2, _, _, _) and
            trainingCourse(CID2, _, _, AID2) and AID1 <> AID2 ) };
```

√Q5: Which employees have the minimum salary?

```
(eID, eLast, eFirst, eTitle, eSalary)

{ EID, ELast, EFirst, ETitle, ESalary |
    employee(EID, ELast, EFirst, ETitle, ESalary) and
    not (exists Salary) (employee(_, _, _, _, Salary) and
        Salary < ESalary) };
```

√Q6: Which employees took all of the training courses offered in the Database technology area?

```
(eID, eLast, eFirst, eTitle)

{ EID, ELast, EFirst, ETitle |
    employee(EID, ELast, EFirst, ETitle, _) and
    dbEmployee(EID, _, _, _) and
    not (exists DBCourse)
        (dbCourse(DBCourse, _, _) and
        not takes(EID, DBCourse, _, _, _) ) };
```

3.4 BY-NAME SYNTAX

The by-position syntax of theoretical DRC provides a useful language for declaratively specifying the properties of the data to be retrieved by a query. Variables ranging over the domains of attributes provide inherent support for the specification of equality constraints between attributes of different tables by using the same variable name. An equality constraint between an attribute and a domain constant is also inherent by using the domain constant to reference the attribute directly. However, there is a disadvantage to this positional syntax. The query composer must know the position of the attributes within each table in the relational database schema. A by-name syntax, such as that offered by relational algebra, does not require the knowledge of the position of the attribute within the table but only the name of the attribute.

Consider the following by-name version of query Q1, which finds the training courses offered in the database technology area:

```
dbCourse(cID:C, cTitle:T, cHours:H) ← (exists A)
    (technologyArea(aTitle:'Database', aID:A) and
    trainingCourse(areaID:A, cID:C, cTitle:T, cHours:H));
```

This by-name syntax makes the schema of the resulting table explicit by declaring the attribute names and associating a domain variable with each attribute.[1] These global domain variables (`C, T`, and `H`) must appear in a positive atom within the expression to return the query bindings. The pragmatic symbol (←) is used instead of the theoretical notation (|) to separate the free variables from the query expression. The attributes of the `technologyArea` and `trainingCourse` tables are referenced by name. The domain constant `'Database'` constrains the value of the `aTitle` attribute of `technologyArea`. The local domain variable `A` references both the `aID` attribute of `technologyArea` and the `areaID` attribute of `trainingCourse` to perform a natural join of the two tables. The global variables are bound by their appearance in the reference to the `trainingCourse` table.

3.5 SUMMARY

The DRC language is relationally complete and provides an equivalent declarative specification of a relational algebra expression. The DRC language has a *by-position syntax*, referencing an attribute by its position in the tuple of a relation. Since the variables of the DRC language range over domains of attributes of relations, the language allows for several pragmatic shortcuts:

- The use of anonymous variables (_) to hold the position of an attribute whose value is not explicitly referenced.
- The ability to constrain the value of an attribute to that of a domain constant by referencing the attribute directly using the domain constant.
- The inherent support for the specification of equality constraints between attributes of different tables by using the same variable name, such as in a natural join or intersection.

Although the theoretical DRC language has a by-position syntax, the pragmatic by-name syntax presented is preferable, as it alleviates the need for the use of anonymous variables, while preserving the other shortcuts of the language.

[1]This syntax is loosely based on the Datalog Extended Language (DEL) of the VALIDITY commercial deductive object-oriented database system. (See bibliographic notes for more information.)

DISCUSSION

The declarative approach to the query specification in DRC is a definite paradigm shift from the procedural approach of relational algebra. Some may prefer a declarative approach to an imperative one: others prefer the opposite. Consider the example EMPLOYEE TRAINING queries illustrating various types of queries that were presented in both relational algebra and DRC. Queries Q1, Q2, and Q3 appear relatively straightforward in both languages. Since these formal languages do not support aggregation, the algebra and DRC solutions for Q4 and Q5 are creative. One may argue that the inventive solutions of DRC for Q4 and Q5 are more elegant than those specified in relational algebra. Yet others may debate that the division query of Q6 is easier to understand procedurally in relational algebra than declaratively in DRC.

The procedural operations of relational algebra are critical in understanding the operations involved in retrieving data from a relational database. This imperative approach provides a useful formalism for the optimization of queries. The declarative query languages, however, provide an alternative approach to specifying the properties of the data to be retrieved rather than specifying how to retrieve the data. The declarative specification of queries is the basis of SQL. The syntax of the basic query expression in SQL is a variation of tuple relational calculus, which is the query language described in the next chapter.

EXERCISES

Most of the DRC queries presented in this chapter were answered in one step. You may use intermediate tables to break down a query into logical units. However, it is strongly suggested that you do not attempt a translation of your relational algebra solutions to DRC. Therefore, different exercises on the EMPLOYEE TRAINING *schema are given to encourage declarative thinking.*

√ Use the WinRDBI educational tool to *check* the answers to these marked exercises.

√3.1 Answer the following queries in DRC over the EMPLOYEE TRAINING schema:

```
employee(eID, eLast, eFirst, eTitle, eSalary)
technologyArea(aID, aTitle, aURL, aLeadID)
trainingCourse(cID, cTitle, cHours, areaID)
takes(eID, cID, tYear, tMonth, tDay)
```

(a) Which training courses are offered in a given month?

Look at the database instance, and choose a month and year that will not yield an empty result.

```
(cID, cTitle, cHours, aTitle)
```

(b) Which employee leads have not taken a training course in the technology area that they lead?

```
(eID, eLast, eFirst, eTitle, aTitle)
```

(c) Which employees took *only one* course in the 'Java' technology area?

```
(eID, eLast, eFirst, eTitle)
```

(d) Which training courses have the minimum number of hours?

```
(cID, cTitle, cHours, aTitle)
```

(e) Which coaches have taken *all* of the courses in the 'Java' technology area?

```
(eID, eLast, eFirst, eTitle)
```

√**3.2** Answer Exercise 2.1 in DRC. Do not translate the relational algebra solutions to DRC! Verify that you obtained the same set of results on the same database instance for each query. Compare your DRC solutions with those you found with relational algebra. Which paradigm do you prefer on what types of queries?

√**3.3** Answer Exercise 2.2 in DRC. Verify your results and compare your solutions.

3.4 The most common mistake in constructing a division query in DRC is the lack of use of the implication within the universally quantified formula.

```
{ A | abTable(A, _) and (forall B) (bTable(B) and abTable(A,B) ) }
```

(a) Construct the truth table for the preceding *incorrect* specification of the division query. Compare the truth table you obtained with the one given in Table 3.4.

(b) Use the logical equivalences to convert the universally quantified formula to an existentially quantified one.

POSTSCRIPT

Once you have answered Exercise 3.1 in DRC, you may want to answer the queries of Exercise 3.1 in relational algebra. Again, verify your results, and compare your solutions. Did the paradigm shift from declarative to procedural change the manner in which you approached the relational algebra queries?

Chapter 4

Tuple Relational Calculus

TRC is important to understand, because the heart of SQL is a syntactic variation of TRC; this will be illustrated in the next chapter on SQL. The variables of the TRC language range over tuples of relations, instead of the domains of attributes as in DRC, which was described in the previous chapter. TRC is also a relationally complete language, which is illustrated by the examples based on the fundamental and additional operators of relational algebra over the EMPLOYEE TRAINING enterprise. Over the same enterprise, six example queries highlight the similarities and differences of the declarative relational calculus languages over various types of queries.

4.1 EXPRESSIONS

The TRC expressions[1] defined here follow the conventions previously adopted in this book: Identifiers starting with a lowercase letter denote relation and attribute names, identifiers that begin with an uppercase letter denote variables (in this case, tuple variables), and constants are either single-quoted strings or numeric constants. To refer to the name of an attribute associated with a tuple variable, dot notation is used. For example, `T.a` refers to the attribute `a` of the tuple variable `T`. The identifiers

[1]Most textbooks do not provide definitions of expressions in both relational calculus languages and instead rely on the reader to make the assumption of the definition of one relational calculus language from the other. This book chooses to state the perhaps straightforward definition of TRC expressions to give the reader the freedom to read the TRC chapter without having to read the DRC chapter first, although the reader is encouraged to do so.

`not, and, or, exists,` and `forall` are used instead of the mathematical symbols denoting negation ($\neg$), conjunction ($\wedge$), disjunction ($\vee$), existential quantification ($\exists$), and universal quantification ($\forall$), respectively.

A general TRC expression is of the form

$$\{ \text{T1}, \text{T2}, \ldots, \text{Tn} \mid \mathcal{F}(\text{T1}, \text{T2}, \ldots, \text{Tn}) \},$$

where $\mathcal{F}$ is a TRC formula describing the properties that are to hold true on the data to be retrieved. The output schema of $\mathcal{F}$ is given by the attributes associated with the tuple variables T1, T2, . . . , Tn.

The building block of a TRC formula is an atom consisting of a reference to a relation or a comparison of an attribute of a tuple variable to an attribute of another tuple variable or a domain constant. An atom forms the basis of a formula, which is built up from atoms using logical connectives (`not, and, or`) and quantification (`exists, forall`).

Let

`r` be a relation of degree n
`T` and `Ti` represent tuple variables
`ai` represent an attribute
`c` be a domain constant
θ be a comparison operator (<, =<, =, >, >=, <>), and assume that its operands are comparable by θ

An atom is of the form

- `r(T)`
  TRUE when T is assigned a value forming a tuple in `r`.
- `Ti.am` θ `Tj.an`
  TRUE when `Ti.am` θ `Tj.an` is TRUE and otherwise FALSE.
- `T.ai` θ `c`
  TRUE when `T.ai` θ `c` is TRUE and otherwise FALSE.

A formula is composed of atoms using the following rules:

(1) An atom is a formula.
Its meaning is given by the truth value of the atom.

(2) Let $\mathcal{F}$, $\mathcal{F}1$, and $\mathcal{F}2$ be formulas; then the following are formulas:

- ($\mathcal{F}$)
  TRUE when $\mathcal{F}$ is TRUE and otherwise FALSE.
- `not` $\mathcal{F}$
  TRUE when $\mathcal{F}$ is FALSE and otherwise FALSE.

- $\mathcal{F}1$ and $\mathcal{F}2$
  TRUE when both $\mathcal{F}1$ and $\mathcal{F}2$ are TRUE and otherwise FALSE.
- $\mathcal{F}1$ or $\mathcal{F}2$
  TRUE when either $\mathcal{F}1$ or $\mathcal{F}2$ are TRUE and otherwise FALSE.

(3) Let $\mathcal{F}(T)$ be a formula in which the variable T appears free. A variable is free if it is not quantified by an existential or universal quantifier. Then the following are formulas:

- `(exists T)`$\mathcal{F}(T)$
  TRUE if there exists a value assigned to T that makes $\mathcal{F}(T)$ TRUE and otherwise FALSE.
- `(forall T)`$\mathcal{F}(T)$
  TRUE if any value that is assigned to T makes $\mathcal{F}(T)$ TRUE and otherwise FALSE.

A valid TRC expression $\{T1, T2, \ldots, Tn \mid \mathcal{F}(T1, T2, \ldots, Tn)\}$ has only the tuple variables $T1, T2, \ldots, Tn$ free in $\mathcal{F}$. Free variables are global variables with respect to the TRC expression $\mathcal{F}$. Any other variable appearing in $\mathcal{F}$ is a local variable and is bound by its quantified declaration. The scope of the local variable is the quantified formula. The remainder of the chapter illustrates the TRC language by example.

The result of a TRC expression may be saved in an intermediate table. The syntax

```
intermediateTable := queryExpression;
```

assigns the result of the `queryExpression` to the `intermediateTable`. The attribute names for the schema of `intermediateTable` are derived from the `queryExpression`. However, if renaming of attributes is desired, then the syntax

```
intermediateTable(attr1, ..., attrn) := queryExpression;
```

provides for the renaming of the output schema of `queryExpression` to the schema given by the attribute list `attr1, ..., attrn`.

4.2 EXPRESSIVE POWER

Like DRC, the TRC language is relationally complete, since any relational algebra query can be expressed in TRC. The TRC language is introduced using the examples over the EMPLOYEE TRAINING enterprise, first illustrating the relational completeness of TRC using the fundamental operators and then describing the additional operators of relational algebra in TRC. In the examples, the names of the tuple variables are usually abbreviated to one or two characters, based on a mnemonic association with the table over which the tuple variable ranges. For the EMPLOYEE TRAINING enterprise examples, the following tuple variable naming convention is used:

- `E` refers to the `employee` relation.
- `T` refers to the `takes` relation.
- `A` refers to the `technologyArea` relation.
- `C` refers to the `trainingCourse` relation.

Although more descriptive tuple variable names are possible, this naming convention for tuple variables provides concise, yet readable, examples.

4.2.1 Fundamental Operators

Table 4.1 summarizes the TRC expressions for operations involving the fundamental relational algebra operators, which identify the required operations for effective retrieval of information from a relational database.

The examples over the EMPLOYEE TRAINING enterprise that illustrate the expression of the fundamental operators in TRC are summarized in Table 4.2.

TABLE 4.1 TRC summary of fundamental relational algebra operators.

Algebra	TRC
σ_θ(r)	{ R | r(R) and θ }
π_A(r)	{ R.ai . . . R.aj | r(R) }
r ∪ s	{ T | r(T) or s(T) }
r − s	{ T | r(T) and not s(T) }
q × r	{ Q, R | q(Q) and r(R) }

TABLE 4.2 TRC summary of fundamental EMPLOYEE TRAINING queries.

Query	√TRC
Q_σ	{ E | employee(E) and E.eSalary > 100000 };
Q_π	{ E.eLast, E.eFirst, E.eTitle | employee(E)};
$Q_\cup$	managers := { E.eID | employee(E) and E.eTitle='Manager' }; coaches := { E.eID | employee(E) and E.eTitle='Coach' }; { T | managers(T) or coaches(T) };
Q_-	managers := { E.eID | employee(E) and E.eTitle='Manager' }; takenCourse := { T.eID | takes(T) }; { T | managers(T) and not takenCourse(T) };
$Q_\times$	{ E.eID, C.cID | employee(E) and trainingCourse(C) };

Query Q_σ:

```
√ { E | employee(E) and E.eSalary > 100000 };
```

The tuple variable E is the only variable that appears in the TRC formula. This variable is a free or global variable, since it is not quantified within the TRC formula. The atom `employee(E)` binds the variable E to a tuple in the `employee` relation. The atom `E.eSalary > 100000` then checks whether the employee's salary is greater than 100000. The output schema of the TRC expression consists of the attributes associated with the tuple variable E, which are the attributes of the table `employee(eID, eLast, eFirst, eTitle, eSalary)`.

Query Q_π:

```
√ { E.eLast, E.eFirst, E.eTitle | employee(E)};
```

Dot notation projects the desired attributes of the tuple variable E that ranges over the `employee` table.

Query $Q_\cup$:

```
√   managers :=
      { E.eID | employee(E) and E.eTitle='Manager' };
    coaches :=
      { E.eID | employee(E) and E.eTitle='Coach' };
    { T | managers(T) or coaches(T) };
```

The first expression finds the identification number of employees who are managers, using the global or free tuple variable E to range over the employee table, and then the value of the `eTitle` determines whether the employee is a manager. Similarly, the second expression finds the identification number of employees who are coaches. The third expression unions the compatible intermediate tables `managers` or `coaches`. The tuple variable T is free in the union TRC expression, getting its bindings from the operands of the disjunction. Therefore, the disjuncts of a valid disjunctive expression must have the same free variables.

Although the previous specification of the query used the general template for expressing a union in TRC, the query can be specified in one step:

```
√ { E.eID | employee(E) and
     (E.eTitle = 'Manager' or E.eTitle = 'Coach') };
```

Query Q_-:

```
√   managers :=
      { E.eID | employee(E) and E.eTitle='Manager' };
    takenCourse := { T.eID | takes(T) };
    { T | managers(T) and not takenCourse(T) };
```

The first intermediate table managers contains the eID of employees having the title Manager. The second intermediate table takenCourse contains the eID of employees that have taken a course, as given by the takes tables. The answer to the query returns the set of tuples T such that T forms a tuple in the managers table and does not form a tuple in the takenCourse table. An alternative specification of the query can be given as a single query:

```
√  { E.eID | employee(E) and E.eTitle='Manager' and
     not (exists T) (takes(T) and T.eID=E.eID) };
```

In this version of the query, the tuple variable E is a global variable, and T is a local variable, defined only within the scope of the negated formula.

Query $Q_{\times}$:

```
√  { E.eID, C.cID | employee(E) and trainingCourse(C) };
```

The simplifying assumption for the cartesian product operator in relational algebra requires that the operand relations do not have any attributes in common. In the TRC language, the same assumption for the result of a cartesian product must hold. The resulting relation schema must not contain duplicate attribute names. The specification of the query $Q_{\times}$ represents a cartesian product of the employee and trainingCourse tables in TRC. The eID and cID attributes of the tuple variables E and C, respectively, are specified as the result of the query to be consistent with the schema of the corresponding relational algebra example.

4.2.2 Additional Operators

Table 4.3 summarizes the illustrative examples over the EMPLOYEE TRAINING enterprise using the additional binary operators of relational algebra ($\cap$, $\bowtie_{\theta}$, $\bowtie$), which

TABLE 4.3 TRC summary of additional EMPLOYEE TRAINING queries.

Query	√TRC
$Q_{\cap}$	managers := { E.eID | employee(E) and E.eTitle='Manager' }; takenCourse := { T.eID | takes(T) }; { T | managers(T) and takenCourse(T) };
$Q_{\bowtie_{\theta}}$	{ E, A | employee(E) and technologyArea(A) and E.eID=A.aLeadID };
$Q_{\bowtie}$	{ C.cTitle, T.tYear, T.tMonth, T.tDay | trainingCourse(C) and takes(T) and C.cID=T.cID };

are frequently used combinations of the fundamental operators. The division (÷) binary operator is not given in the table but delegated to a more detailed discussion later in this section.

Query $Q_{\cap}$:

√
```
managers :=
  { E.eID | employee(E) and E.eTitle='Manager' };
takenCourse := { T.eID | takes(T) };
{ T | managers(T) and takenCourse(T) };
```

The intersection operation is achieved by using the same tuple variable name in both atoms referencing the operand relations. The query can also be specified in one step:

√
```
{ E.eID | employee(E) and E.eTitle='Manager' and
    (exists T) (takes(T) and T.eID=E.eID) };
```

In this version of the query, the tuple variable E is a global variable, and T is a local variable defined only within the scope of the existential formula.

Query $Q_{\bowtie_\theta}$:

√
```
{ E, A | employee(E) and technologyArea(A) and
    E.eID=A.aLeadID };
```

The global variables E and A range over the tables to be joined. The join condition E.eID=A.aLeadID joins the employee and technologyArea tables such that the employee eID is equal to the aLeadID of the technology area.

Query $Q_{\bowtie}$:

√
```
{ C.cTitle, T.tYear, T.tMonth, T.tDay |
    trainingCourse(C) and takes(T) and C.cID=T.cID };
```

In DRC, using the same domain variable name in the positions that are to be joined results in a natural join. Since there is no shortcut available for the natural join in TRC, the attributes to be joined must be done so explicitly (e.g., C.cID=T.cID).

Division. Division is a complex binary relational algebra operator that finds those values in the first operand relation that are related to *all* of the values in the second operand relation. The same abstract division example (abTable ÷ bTable), where the schemas of the operand relations are abTable(a,b) and bTable(b), demonstrates the expression of division in TRC. This illustration includes the expressibility of division in TRC using both universal and existential quantification, along with their corresponding truth tables.[2]

The abstract division example includes an a value in the result of the division, provided that the a value is in the abTable and for all possible B values, if B is a tuple in the bTable, then the a and b values are related by the abTable:

```
{ T.a | abTable(T) and (forall B) (bTable(B) implies
    (exists AB) (abTable(AB) and AB.a=T.a and AB.b=B.b) ) };
```

Why does the TRC specification look more complicated than its corresponding specification in the DRC language?

```
{ A | abTable(A, _) and (forall B) (bTable(B) implies
    abTable(A,B) ) };
```

This DRC specification is utilizing shortcuts of the DRC language. Without the shortcut, the DRC specification more closely resembles the TRC:

```
{ A | abTable(A, _) and (forall B) (bTable(B) implies
    (exists A1,B1) (abTable(A1,B1) and A1=A and B1=B) ) };
```

Since the implies operator is not formally defined in this version of TRC, the logically equivalent specification using not p or q instead of p implies q is

```
√ { T.a | abTable(T) and (forall B) (not bTable(B) or
      (exists AB) (abTable(AB) and AB.a=T.a and AB.b=B.b) ) };
```

Table 4.4 shows the corresponding truth table. The forall formula must be true for all values of the variable B, including those B values that do not form a tuple in the bTable.

Consider a logically equivalent specification of division that uses only existential quantification. An a value is included in the result of the division, provided that the a value is in the abTable and it is not the case that there exists a b value that is in the bTable and is *not* related to the a value by the abTable:

```
√ { T.a | abTable(T) and not (exists B) (bTable(B) and
      not (exists AB) (abTable(AB) and AB.a=T.a and AB.b=B.b) ) };
```

[2] Although this exposition closely resembles the similar description in DRC, it is included here so that the reader can follow its derivation in terms of TRC.

TABLE 4.4 TRC division: universal truth table.

abTable(T)	b	not bTable(B)	(exists AB)	not bTable(B) or (exists AB)	forall B
(a1)	b1	F	T	T	
	b2	F	T	T	T
	b3	T	F	T	
(a2)	b1	F	F	F	
	b2	F	T	T	F
	b3	T	F	T	
(a3)	b1	F	T	T	
	b2	F	T	T	T
	b3	T	T	T	

This logically equivalent existential specification can be derived from the universal specification using the following logical equivalences:

- Given the universal specification

```
√ { T.a | abTable(T) and (forall B) (not bTable(B) or
      (exists AB) (abTable(AB) and AB.a=T.a and AB.b=B.b) ) };
```

- Apply the logical equivalence: `(forall D)` $\mathcal{F}$`(D)` $\equiv$ `not (exists D) not` $\mathcal{F}$`(D)`

```
√ { T.a | abTable(T) and not (exists B) not (not bTable(B) or
      (exists AB) (abTable(AB) and AB.a=T.a and AB.b=B.b) ) };
```

- Apply DeMorgan's Law: `not (p or q)` $\equiv$ `not p and not q`

```
√ { T.a | abTable(T) and not (exists B) (bTable(B) and
      not (exists AB) (abTable(AB) and AB.a=T.a
      and AB.b=B.b) ) };
```

Table 4.5 shows the corresponding truth table.

4.2.3 Safety

By illustrating how the operators of relational algebra can be expressed in TRC, the previous examples have demonstrated the relational completeness of TRC. Although the result of a relational algebra expression is finite, not all TRC expressions produce a finite result. Consider the TRC expression that attempts to find employees who do not lead a technology area, and assume that there exists an intermediate table `leads` containing the IDs of the employees that lead technology areas:

```
{ E | not leads(E) }
```

TABLE 4.5 TRC division: existential truth table.

abTable(T)	b	bTable(B)	not (exists AB)	bTable(B) and not (exists AB)	not (exists B)
(a1)	b1	T	F	F	
	b2	T	F	F	T
	b3	F	T	F	
(a2)	b1	T	T	T	
	b2	T	F	F	F
	b3	F	T	F	
(a3)	b1	T	F	F	
	b2	T	F	F	T
	b3	F	F	F	

There are infinitely many tuple values that are not in the `leads` table. To find those employees who do not lead a technology area, first limit the tuple variable `E` to values of the `employee` table and then check whether the employee ID value appears in the `leads` table:

```
√   { E | employee(E) and not (exists L)
        (leads(L) and L.eID=E.eID) };
```

A *safe* TRC expression guarantees a finite result by limiting (either directly or indirectly) the values of a tuple variable (T) by its appearance in a positive atom (`r(T)`). The Employee Training examples illustrating the relational completeness of the TRC language are safe. Only *safe* TRC expressions can be realized in relational algebra. Therefore, relational algebra and safe TRC (and safe DRC) are equivalent in expressive power.

4.3 EXAMPLE QUERIES

The example queries over the Employee Training enterprise illustrate various types of relevant queries and the use of the TRC language to express these queries. Similar to DRC, the TRC language examples use the convention to limit a variable before its value is referenced in a left-to-right reading of the relational calculus expression. Since safe TRC is equivalent in expressive power to relational algebra and safe DRC, TRC does not support aggregation. Therefore, queries Q4 and Q5 must be answered creatively. The inventive solutions for these queries are similar in concept to the DRC solutions. By finding employees who took two courses from two different technology areas, query Q4 retrieves the employees who took courses in more than one technology area. Query Q5 finds the minimum salary employees by selecting those employees that do not have a salary that is greater than another employee's salary. The division query Q6 finds the employees who have taken at least one course in the database technology area and have taken all database courses. The verification of taking at least one database course is required to produce correct results when the dbCourse table is empty.

√Q1: What training courses are offered in the 'Database' technology area?

```
(cID, cTitle, cHours)

dbCourse :=
 { T.cID, T.cTitle, T.cHours | trainingCourse(T) and (exists A)
   (technologyArea(A) and A.aID = T.areaID and
   A.aTitle = 'Database') };
```

√Q2: Which employees have taken a training course offered in the 'Database' technology area?

```
(eID, eLast, eFirst, eTitle)

dbEmployee :=
{ E.eID, E.eLast, E.eFirst, E.eTitle | employee(E) and
        (exists T,D) (takes(T) and dbCourse(D) and
        T.eID=E.eID and T.cID=D.cID) };
```

√Q3: Which employees have not taken any training courses?

```
(eID, eLast, eFirst, eTitle)

{ E.eID, E.eLast, E.eFirst, E.eTitle | employee(E) and
    not (exists T) (takes(T) and T.eID=E.eID) };
```

√Q4: Which employees took courses in more than one technology area?

```
(eID, eLast, eFirst, eTitle)

{ E.eID, E.eLast, E.eFirst, E.eTitle |
    employee(E) and (exists T1,T2,C1,C2)
        (takes(T1) and T1.eID=E.eID and
        takes(T2) and T2.eID=E.eID and
        trainingCourse(C1) and T1.cID=C1.cID and
        trainingCourse(C2) and T2.cID=C2.cID and
        C1.areaID <> C2.areaID) };
```

√Q5: Which employees have the minimum salary?

```
(eID, eLast, eFirst, eTitle, eSalary)

{ E | employee(E) and
    not (exists S) (employee(S) and S.eSalary < E.eSalary) };
```

√Q6: Which employees took all of the training courses offered in the 'Database' technology area?

```
(eID, eLast, eFirst, eTitle)

{ E.eID, E.eLast, E.eFirst, E.eTitle | employee(E) and
    (exists B)(dbEmployee(B) and B.eID=E.eID) and
    not (exists D)(dbCourse(D) and
        not (exists T) (takes(T) and T.eID=E.eID and
        T.cID=D.cID) ) };
```

4.4 SUMMARY

TRC is a relationally complete language that declaratively specifies the properties of the data to be retrieved, not how to retrieve the data. The variables of the TRC language range over tuples of relations, and the names of attributes associated with the tuple are referenced using dot notation. The TRC *by-name* syntax forms the foundation of SQL, which is described in the next chapter.

DISCUSSION

Some may prefer the TRC *by-name* syntax over the positional syntax offered by the theoretical DRC. However, TRC appears somewhat verbose when compared with DRC. DRC offers pragmatic shortcuts for equality constraints at the domain level, such as natural joins and domain constants. The only shortcut available in both TRC and DRC is the ability to use the same variable names in compatible operations, such as union, difference, and intersection.

EXERCISES

Don't forget that you may use intermediate tables to break down a query into multiple steps. Since TRC and DRC are similar languages, the first exercise presents new queries over the EMPLOYEE TRAINING *schema to encourage the development of TRC expressions that are not based on existing DRC solutions.*

√ Use the WinRDBI educational tool to *check* the answers to these marked exercises.

√4.1 Answer the following queries in TRC over the EMPLOYEE TRAINING schema:

```
employee(eID, eLast, eFirst, eTitle, eSalary)
technologyArea(aID, aTitle, aURL, aLeadID)
trainingCourse(cID, cTitle, cHours, areaID)
takes(eID, cID, tYear, tMonth, tDay)
```

(a) Which employees took training courses in a given month?

Look at the database instance and choose a month and year that will not yield an empty result:

```
(eID, eLast, eFirst, eTitle)
```

(b) Which employees have not taken all of the training courses in the 'Database' technology area?

```
(eID, eLast, eFirst, eTitle)
```

(c) Which employee leads have taken more than one training course in the technology area that they lead?

```
(eID, eLast, eFirst, eTitle)
```

(d) Which training courses in the 'Database' technology area have the maximum number of hours?

```
(cID, cTitle, cHours)
```

(e) Which employees have taken *all* training courses offered in the year 2001?

```
(eID, eLast, eFirst, eTitle)
```

√4.2 Answer Exercise 3.1 in TRC. Do not translate the DRC solutions to TRC! Verify that you obtained the same set of results on the same database instance for each query. Compare your TRC solutions with your DRC solutions. Do you prefer one relational calculus language to the other? Why?

√4.3 Answer Exercise 2.1 in TRC. Verify your results and compare your solutions.

√4.4 Answer Exercise 2.2 in TRC. Verify your results and compare your solutions.

4.5 The most common mistake in constructing a division query in TRC is the lack of use of the implication within the universally quantified formula. Consider the following specification of the division query:

```
{ T.a | abTable(T) and (forall B) (bTable(B) and
    (exists AB) (abTable(AB) and AB.a=T.a and AB.b=B.b) ) }
```

(a) Construct the truth table for the preceding *incorrect* specification of the division query. Compare the truth table you obtained with the one given in Table 4.4.

(b) Use the logical equivalences to convert the universally quantified formula to an existentially quantified one.

POSTSCRIPT

After answering Exercise 4.1 in TRC, you should answer the same queries in relational algebra and DRC. Verify your results, and compare your solutions.

Chapter 5

SQL

SQL is also a declarative query language, which indicates the properties of the data to be retrieved. The basic query expression in SQL is a syntactic variation of an expression in TRC and is easily mapped to its equivalent relational algebra expression. Since SQL is an industry-standard query language, it must be relationally complete. This text illustrates the relational completeness of SQL by providing the SQL expressions for the same queries that illustrated the fundamental and additional operators of relational algebra. The examples over the EMPLOYEE TRAINING enterprise continue to use basic features of SQL to illustrate the relationship between SQL and the formal query languages. For pragmatic reasons, SQL is more powerful than its formal counterparts on which it is based. These additional features of SQL, including ordering and aggregation of results, are illustrated by example. The SQL standard evolved to provide more than a query language, including a DDL, a DML, and a data control language (DCL) for integrity and security.

The SQL standard, originally adopted by the American National Standards Institute (ANSI) in 1986 and the International Standards Organization (ISO) in 1987, contains many components and continues to evolve, with additional versions ratified in 1989, 1992, and 1999. The latest standard SQL:1999 includes support for object-oriented extensions of the relational model, including user-defined data types and object tables, but is beyond the scope of this book, which focuses only on the pure relational model. The 1989 and 1992 standards, SQL-89 and SQL-92, respectively, extended the original standard with various features, which are too numerous to mention in their entirety here. However, the programmatic interfaces to SQL were primarily defined in these revisions to the standard. Since SQL is not a general-purpose programming language, the standard requires that an implementation of SQL support at least one method by which SQL can be invoked programmatically, such as a module, embedded SQL, the Call-Level Interface, and direct SQL. Since the focus of this book is on query languages, this chapter does not cover the programmatic interfaces to SQL, but provides an overview of the ad hoc capabilities of SQL. In general, this overview is compatible with the SQL-92 standard, although the chapter coverage chooses to start with basic SQL query expressions and extends the coverage to include the explicit support for joins, which was added to the standard in SQL-92.

5.1 BASIC QUERY EXPRESSIONS

Although there are always slight variations of the dialect of SQL provided by a given system, the SQL standard provides a description of the language that allows for the portability of database applications. Identifiers in the SQL standard are limited to a maximum of 128 characters; the first character of an identifier must be a letter (upper- or lowercase) and the remaining may be any letter, digit, or underscore. Identifiers are case insensitive in SQL, so the identifiers `tableName` and `tablename` are considered identical. Thus, the syntax conventions for identifiers used in this book are not inconsistent with the SQL standard. Specifically, the SQL examples continue to use identifiers starting with a lowercase letter to refer to the name of a relation or attribute.

The basic SQL query expression selects a list of attributes from relations where a condition holds:

```
select a1, a2, ..., aj
from   r1, r2, ..., rk
where  θ
```

This basic SQL query expression is essentially equivalent to the relational algebra expression

$$\pi_{a1,a2,\ldots,aj}(\sigma_\theta(r1 \times r2 \times \ldots \times rk)).$$

The `select` clause *projects* the desired attributes `from` the cartesian product of the tables that satisfy the *selection* condition specified by the `where` clause. It is interesting to note that the SQL `select` clause is in fact a relational algebra *projection* and not a *selection*. Another point of interest to note is that the `from` clause represents a *cartesian product* of the tables specified. One of the most common mistakes in SQL is not realizing that the `from` clause provides all possible combinations of the tuples from the tables specified in the list. If a relational algebra *join* is desired, then the join condition is specified as part of the `where` clause, which performs a selection on the result of the cartesian product.[1]

[1] SQL-92 introduced a *join* syntax in the `from` clause, which will be described later in this chapter.

There are slight variations on this SQL syntax. If all attributes are desired in the result, an asterisk (*) provides a convenient shorthand:

```
select *
from   r1, r2, ..., rk
where  θ
```

If there is no selection condition, the `where` clause is optional:

```
select *
from   r1, r2, ..., rk
```

The equivalence of the basic SQL expression to its corresponding relational algebra expression was qualified as *essentially equivalent*. The relational algebra and relational calculus languages assume that relations are *sets* of tuples. A set is a collection of elements without duplicates. Therefore, the formal languages implicitly remove duplicate tuples from the result set. However, SQL assumes that a relation is a *multiset*, or *bag*, of tuples, which is a collection of elements that may contain duplicates. Since there is a cost associated with performing duplicate elimination, SQL chooses as a default to keep duplicate tuples. Duplicate elimination is possible using the keyword `distinct` in the select clause:

```
select distinct a1, a2, ..., aj
from   r1, r2, ..., rk
where  θ
```

There are also circumstances that require the use of multisets. Consider the situation where the sum of the salaries of employees is needed to determine the salary budget for a company. If the sum is to be performed on a set of employee salaries, rather than a multiset of salaries, then the result of the sum on the set would be incorrect if there were employees earning the same salary.

This basic SQL query expression is a syntactic variation of the TRC expression:

```
{R1, R2, ..., RK|r1(R1) and r2(R2) and ...rk(Rk) and θ}
```

In the TRC expression, the tuple variables to the left of the vertical bar correspond to the SQL `select` clause, specifying the schema of the resulting relation. The tables in the SQL `from` clause correspond to the table references listed to the right of the vertical bar, which specifies that `Ri` is a tuple variable ranging over the table `ri`. The condition of the `where` clause, denoted θ, is part of the condition of the TRC expression.

In this brief comparison of TRC versus SQL, the differences appear minor. The TRC shortcut for including all attributes appearing in the query expression is to list all of the tuple variables, whereas SQL uses an asterisk. When all attributes corresponding to a tuple variable are not desired, dot notation `T.a` projects the attribute a associated with the tuple variable T. The foregoing SQL syntax shows a list of attribute names. However, since attribute names are only unique within a table, a reference to an attribute name may be ambiguous. SQL also allows the use of dot notation to refer to an attribute and requires dot notation when an attribute reference is ambiguous. For example, if two tables t1 and t2 both contain the attribute a, then the select clause in the following query contains an ambiguous reference to the attribute a:

```
select a
from   t1, t2
where  . . .
```

However, dot notation t1.a disambiguates the reference by specifying the table of the desired attribute:

```
select t1.a
from   t1, t2
where  . . .
```

SQL allows for the specification of *table aliases* for a table in the from clause. There are several reasons for introducing table aliases. One reason is to provide a short name to reference tables, as in the following:

```
select T1.a, T2.b
from   longTableName1 T1, longTableName2 T2
where  . . .
```

Another reason is to provide a mechanism by which the same table can be accessed more than once in the same query. These table aliases (sometimes called *range variables*) play a similar role to the tuple variables in TRC. This similarity will be made obvious in the examples describing the SQL language by following the same conventions that were used for describing the TRC language. For example, the identifiers used to denote the preceding table aliases begin with an uppercase letter, as was done in TRC.

For consistency of presentation of the query languages, the examples illustrating SQL also assume the same syntax for intermediate tables and renaming of attributes:

```
intermediateTable(attr1, . . ., attrn) := queryExpression;
```

If renaming of attributes is not desired, the syntax

```
intermediateTable := queryExpression;
```

derives the attribute names for the schema of intermediateTable from the queryExpression. SQL has its own syntax for defining tables and renaming attributes, which is introduced later in this chapter.

5.2 EXPRESSIVE POWER

SQL is relationally complete, and following the explanation of the other query languages, this section gives a corresponding SQL query expression for the fundamental and additional operators of relational algebra. The focus of this exposition is on the expressive power of the basic SQL expression to emphasize the correlation between SQL and TRC. To make this relationship more obvious, the examples use mnemonic table aliases that are identifiers starting with an uppercase letter similar to that of TRC. Also, a table alias is often used to refer to an attribute, even when it is not necessary to disambiguate the attribute reference.

5.2.1 Fundamental Operators

A relationally complete language must provide at least the equivalence of the fundamental relational algebra operators (σ, π, $\cup$, $-$, $\times$). Table 5.1 summarizes the SQL expressions for abstract operations involving the fundamental relational algebra operators.

TABLE 5.1 SQL summary of fundamental relational algebra operators.

Algebra	SQL
σ_θ(r)	select * from r where θ
π_A(r)	select distinct A from r
r $\cup$ s	select * from r union select * from s
r $-$ s	select * from r except select * from s
q $\times$ r	select * from q, r

Table 5.2 provides the SQL queries that correspond to the illustrative examples over the EMPLOYEE TRAINING enterprise using the fundamental operators. Query Q_σ is a straightforward selection of an `employee` having a salary greater than \$100,000.

Query Q_π projects the desired attributes of the table alias `E` that ranges over the `employee` table. Since the key attribute `eID` of the `employee` table is not included in the result of the query, duplicates may occur in the result. Therefore, `distinct` is added to the `select` clause to return a *set* of tuples to be equivalent to the relational algebra specification.

Query $Q_\cup$ unions together the SQL query expressions that find employees who are managers and employees who are coaches. Note the SQL queries that are operands of the `union` query are compatible. In general, the union requires that the tables have the same number of attributes and that the types of the attributes are compatible.

TABLE 5.2 SQL summary of fundamental EMPLOYEE TRAINING queries.

Query	√SQL
Q_σ	`select * from employee E where E.eSalary > 100000;`
Q_π	`select distinct E.eLast, E.eFirst, E.eTitle from employee E;`

$Q_\cup$	`select E.eID from employee E where E.eTitle='Manager'`
	`union`
	`select E.eID from employee E where E.eTitle='Coach';`

Q_-	`select E.eID from employee E where E.eTitle='Manager'`
	`except`
	`select T.eID from takes T;`

$Q_\times$	`select E.eID, C.cID from employee E, trainingCourse C ;`

By default, SQL removes duplicate tuples in union queries. To allow duplicates, the option `all` can be specified after the `union`. For example,

```
select * from r union all select * from s
```

If a tuple t appears t_r times in `r` and t_s times in `s`, then t appears $t_r + t_s$ times in the resulting union all. The definition of how an operator deals with duplicates, as just described for the `union all`, is known as its *duplicate semantics*.

The previous version of the "Managers or Coaches" query purposely follows the general template for expressing a union in SQL. However, this particular query can also be phrased as the single query:

√
```
select *
from   employee E
where  E.eTitle = 'Manager' or E.eTitle = 'Coach';
```

Query Q_- uses the `except` operator to return the employees who are managers and have not taken a training course. The `except` operator has similar assumptions to that of the `union` operator on type compatibility and duplicate removal. The option `all` is also available on the `except` operator:

```
select * from r except all select * from s
```

The duplicate semantics of the `except all` for a tuple t appearing t_r times in `r` and t_s times in `s` is the maximum of zero or $t_r - t_s$.

Query $Q_\times$ represents a cartesian product of the `employee` and `trainingCourse` tables. To be consistent with the relational algebra specification for this query, the result of the query includes only the `eID` and `cID` attributes of the table aliases `E` and `C`, respectively. Recall that the simplifying assumption for the cartesian product operator in relational algebra requires that the operand relations not have any attribute names in common, so that the result of the cartesian product does not contain duplicate attribute names. Since the selective renaming of columns in SQL has not yet been introduced, this exposition makes a similar assumption.

5.2.2 Additional Operators

The additional relational algebra operators ($\cap$, $\bowtie_\theta$, $\bowtie$, $\div$) provide an abbreviation for frequently used combinations of the fundamental operators. The SQL queries that correspond to the illustrative examples over the EMPLOYEE TRAINING enterprise using these additional operators of relational algebra are summarized in Table 5.3.

TABLE 5.3 SQL summary of additional EMPLOYEE TRAINING queries.

Query	√SQL

$Q_\cap$	`select E.eID from employee E where E.eTitle='Manager'`
	`intersect`
	`select T.eID from takes T;`

$Q_{\bowtie_\theta}$	`select *`
	`from employee E, technologyArea A`
	`where E.eID=A.aLeadID;`

$Q_\bowtie$	`select distinct C.cTitle, T.tYear, T.tMonth, T.tDay`
	`from trainingCourse C, takes T`
	`where C.cID=T.cID ;`

Query $Q_\cap$ finds the employees who are managers and have taken a training course. The type compatibility and duplicate removal assumptions of the union operator apply to the `intersect` operator, including the `all` option:

```
select * from r intersect all select * from s
```

If a tuple t appears t_r times in `r` and t_s times in `s`, then the duplicate semantics of the `intersect all` results in the tuple t appearing the minimum of t_r or t_s times.

Query $Q_{\bowtie_\theta}$ illustrates a join of the `employee` and `technologyArea` tables such that the employee `eID` is equal to the `aLeadID` of the technology area.

Query $Q_\bowtie$ joins the `trainingCourse` and `takes` tables on the `cID` attributes in the where clause. The `distinct` in the select clause eliminates the many duplicates that otherwise would be included in the result, since the multiset version would include a tuple for each employee taking the course on a given date.

In relational algebra, the natural join ($\bowtie$) provides a convenient shorthand for joining two tables such that the value of attributes with the same name in both operand relations are equal. A projection is automatically introduced to include only one copy of the duplicate attributes. DRC provides a shortcut for natural join by using the same domain variable name in the positions that are to be (natural) joined. Both TRC and the basic SQL query expression do not provide for a natural join shortcut. However, SQL-92 introduced a natural join syntax in the `from` clause, which is described later in this chapter.

The discussion of the relational algebra division operator is deferred to the next section, which introduces exists as part of a conditional expression in SQL, which is essential to the specification of division in SQL.

5.2.3 Exists

The examples thus far illustrate the similarity of the basic SQL query expression to a TRC expression. However, the definition of a TRC formula includes the subformula `(exists T)`$\mathcal{F}$`(T)`, which is TRUE if there exists a value assigned to T that makes $\mathcal{F}$(T) TRUE; otherwise, the subformula is FALSE. SQL also allows for `exists` as part of its conditional expression in the `where` clause. Specifically, the syntax is

`exists` (*table-expression*)

where `exists` is TRUE when the *table-expression* does not result in an empty table; otherwise, the `exists` is FALSE. In the TRC chapter, the `exists` subformula appeared in the examples describing the difference, intersection, and division operators of relational algebra in the context of relational calculus.

Difference. The difference example query over the EMPLOYEE TRAINING enterprise retrieves the identification number of employees who are managers that have *not* taken any training courses. The previous version of the query used the `except` operator in SQL after defining the `managers` and `takenCourse` intermediate tables:

```
select * from managers except select * from takenCourse;
```

This query can also be specified in one step in SQL using an `exists` condition in the `where` clause:

√
```
select E.eID
from   employee E
where  E.eTitle='Manager' and not exists
       (select  *
       from     takes T
       where    T.eID=E.eID);
```

The `select–from–where` table expression appearing in the `where` clause is a nested query, which is nested inside the outer `select–from–where` query. If the nested query returns an empty table, indicating that the employee has not taken a training course, then the `exists` evaluates to FALSE and the `not` evaluates to TRUE. If the conditional `E.eTitle='Manager'` also evaluates to TRUE, then the employee is included in the result of the (outer) query.

This alternative specification of the `except` query is an example of a *nested correlated subquery*. The query `select * from takes T where T.eID=E.eID` is a nested subquery that is correlated by referencing the value of the `eID` attribute of the `employee` table from the outer query within the nested subquery.

Intersection. The intersection example query over the EMPLOYEE TRAINING enterprise retrieves the identification number of employees who are managers and have taken at least one training course:

```
select * from managers intersect select * from takenCourse;
```

The `intersect` query can also be specified in one step using a similar nested correlated subquery:

```
√  select E.eID
   from   employee E
   where  E.eTitle='Manager' and exists
          (select  *
           from    takes T
           where   T.eID=E.eID);
```

In this case, an employee that is a manager is included in the result if there exists a tuple in the `takes` table for that employee.

Division. The division example query over the abstract domain finds the a's from the `abTable` that are related to *all* of the b's specified in the `bTable`, where the schema of the tables are `abTable(a,b)` and `bTable(b)`. Since SQL does not provide for the specification of universal quantification, SQL's specification of division uses the logically equivalent definition in terms of existential quantification:

```
√  select distinct T.a
   from   abTable T
   where  not exists
          (select  *                                      -- β
           from    bTable B
           where   not exists
                   (select  *                             -- αβ
                    from    abTable AB
                    where   AB.a=T.a and AB.b=B.b));
```

This division query finds the a's from the `abTable` such that it is not the case that there exists a `b` value in the `bTable` that is *not* related to the `a` value by the `abTable`. Recall that the instance of `bTable` contains the tuples `{ (b1),(b2) }` and that the instance of `abTable` contains the tuples `{(a1,b1), (a1,b2), (a2,b2), (a3,b1), (a3,b2), (a3,b3)}`. Therefore, the answer to the query is `{(a1),(a3)}`.

Table 5.4 shows a truth table that corresponds to the specification of division in SQL on the abstract example. There are two nested queries in this example, which are labelled by comments in the SQL specification. The innermost nested query $\alpha\beta$ checks whether the `a` value from the outermost query (`T.a`) is related by the `abTable` to the `b` value from the inner query (`B.b`). The nested query β checks whether there exists a `b` value in the `bTable` that is not related by the `abTable` to the a value specified in the outermost query (`T.a`). The truth table indicates that the `a1` and `a3` values from the `abTable` are related to *all* of the values in the `bTable` (i.e., related to `b1` and `b2`). The value `a2` is not included in the result, since there exists a `b` value, specifically `b2`, that is not related to `a2` by the `abTable`.

TABLE 5.4 SQL division truth table.

T.a	B.b	exists $\alpha\beta$	not exists $\alpha\beta$	exists β	not exists β
a1	b1	T	F	F	T
	b2	T	F		
a2	b1	T	F	T	F
	b2	F	T		
a3	b1	T	F	F	T
	b2	T	F		

5.2.4 Safety

The previous examples have demonstrated the relational completeness of SQL, illustrating how the operators of relational algebra can be expressed in SQL. Recall that a *safe* expression guarantees a finite result, and it is well known that relational algebra and safe TRC (and safe DRC) are equivalent in expressive power. Is SQL safe? Yes. The syntax of SQL guarantees the safety of the SQL language. Since an `exists` or `not exists` condition must appear only in a `where` clause that is associated with a (`select` and) `from` clause, a basic SQL query expression limits a table alias to a positive table reference in the `from` clause. The example query over the EMPLOYEE TRAINING enterprise used in the safety discussion for relational calculus languages finds the employees that do not lead technology areas, assuming that there exists an intermediate table `leads` containing the IDs of the employees that lead technology areas:

√
```
select E.eID
from   employee E
where  not exists
       (select  *
        from    leads L
        where   L.eID=E.eID);
```

The table alias `E` is inherently limited to tuples in the employee table and the `eID` attribute is checked in the nested subquery to determine whether the employee leads a technology area.

5.3 EXAMPLE QUERIES

This section illustrates the six Employee Training example queries using the basic SQL query expression, continuing to emphasize its similarity to TRC. For example, queries Q4 and Q5 continue to use the creative relational calculus approach to answer a more than one and minimum query, even though SQL provides inherent support for counting and finding the minimum or maximum. The next section explores the additional capabilities of SQL. In addition to introducing new queries to illustrate these features, we present alternative solutions to queries Q1 through Q5. The approach to answer the division query Q6 is the same in both SQL and TRC: finding an employee who has taken at least one database course and it's not the case that there exists a database course that the employee has not taken.

√Q1: What training courses are offered in the 'Database' technology area?

```
(cID, cTitle, cHours)

dbCourse :=
  select C.cID, C.cTitle, C.cHours
  from   trainingCourse C
  where  exists
         (select *
         from    technologyArea A
         where   A.aID = C.areaID and
                 A.aTitle = 'Database');
```

√Q2: Which employees have taken a training course offered in the 'Database' technology area?

```
(eID, eLast, eFirst, eTitle)

dbEmployee :=
         select  E.eID, E.eLast, E.eFirst, E.eTitle
         from    employee E
         where   exists
                 (select *
                 from    takes T, dbCourse D
                 where   T.eID=E.eID and T.cID=D.cID);
```

√Q3: Which employees have not taken any training courses?

```
(eID, eLast, eFirst, eTitle)

select  E.eID, E.eLast, E.eFirst, E.eTitle
from    employee E
where   not exists
        (select *
        from    takes T
        where   T.eID=E.eID);
```

√Q4: Which employees took courses in more than one technology area?

```
(eID, eLast, eFirst, eTitle)

select  E.eID, E.eLast, E.eFirst, E.eTitle
from    employee E
where   exists
        (select *
        from    takes T1, takes T2,
                trainingCourse C1, trainingCourse C2
        where   T1.eID=E.eID and T2.eID=E.eID and
                T1.cID=C1.cID and T2.cID=C2.cID and
                C1.areaID <> C2.areaID);
```

√Q5: Which employees have the minimum salary?

```
(eID, eLast, eFirst, eTitle, eSalary)

select  E.eID, E.eLast, E.eFirst, E.eTitle, E.eSalary
from    employee E
where   not exists
        (select *
        from    employee S
        where   S.eSalary < E.eSalary);
```

√Q6: Which employees took all of the training courses offered in the 'Database' technology area?

```
(eID, eLast, eFirst, eTitle)

select  E.eID, E.eLast, E.eFirst, E.eTitle
from    employee E
where   exists
                (select *
                from    dbEmployee B
                where   B.eID=E.eID) and
        not exists
                (select *
                from    dbCourse D
                where   not exists
                        (select *
                        from    takes T
                        where   T.eID=E.eID and
                                T.cID=D.cID));
```

5.4 ADDITIONAL FEATURES OF THE QUERY LANGUAGE

Up to this point, this chapter has emphasized the similarity between the basic SQL query expression and the formal TRC language on which it is based. Besides the syntactic variation, the only difference pointed out so far is that the formal languages assume that relations are sets of tuples, whereas SQL assumes that relations are multisets of tuples, which allows duplicates. Since SQL is an industry-standard query language, it was designed to be more powerful than TRC. These additional features of SQL include views or virtual tables, sorting and aggregation of results, nested subqueries involving equality and set comparisons, and the flexibility added to the query language in SQL-92 for using joined tables in the `from` clause.

5.4.1 Views and Renaming of Attributes

Throughout the chapters of this text, intermediate tables with optional renaming of attributes provide a mechanism to break down a query into logical pieces. A similar level of abstraction is built into the SQL language as *views* or *virtual tables*. For example, the view `leadsArea` gives the identification number of employees with the technology area that the employee leads:

```
create  view leadsArea as
select  aLeadID, aID
from    technologyArea
```

Both of the definitions of intermediate tables and virtual tables relate a table expression to a table name. However, there is a fundamental difference between intermediate tables and views. When an intermediate table is defined, its defining expression is executed, and the resulting tuples are stored. If the tables appearing in the defining expression change after the intermediate table is defined, the intermediate table will not reflect these changes. In contrast, when a view is defined, its defining expression is stored and executed each time the view is referenced. Therefore, the view will always reflect any changes in the tables appearing in the defining expression. There is, however, a trade-off between the recomputation of a view on each reference versus the inability of an intermediate table to reflect changes from tables in its defining expression.

SQL also supports a concept similar to an intermediate table by its insert data manipulation statement, which allows for the specification of a table expression as the source of the insertion for a named table. A detailed example is provided in the section covering SQL's data manipulation language.

The `leadsArea` virtual table derives the names of the attributes from its defining expression. However, the `create view` statement supports an optional commalist for the renaming of attributes. For example,

```
create  view leadsArea(leadID, areaID) as
select  aLeadID, aID
from    technologyArea
```

renames the `aLeadID` attribute to `leadID` and the `aID` attribute to `areaID`.

Similar to the earlier syntax for renaming attributes while defining an intermediate table, the optional commalist specifies all attributes in the table's schema. However, SQL also supports selective column renaming in the `select` clause.

```
create  view leadsArea as
select  aLeadID, aID as areaID
from    technologyArea
```

In this example, the schema of the view is `leadsArea(aLeadID, areaID)`, where the name of the first attribute `aLeadID` is derived from the expression and the name of the second column is explicitly renamed to `areaID`. This capability of SQL for selective column renaming in the `select` clause is quite useful. Additional examples of the use of selective column renaming in queries that aggregate results appear later in this chapter.

5.4.2 Sorting

The query languages assume that relations are sets or multisets of tuples, which implies an unordered collection of tuples. However, it is quite useful in practice to display the results of a query in a particular order. SQL provides an `order by` clause for that purpose. For example, the following query displays employee information ordered by the employee's last name:

```
√ 01: select     E.eLast, E.eTitle, E.eSalary
      from       employee E
      order by   E.eLast;
```

The `order by` clause also allows for the ordering of multiple attributes and for the specification of the sort order as ascending or descending. In the previous query, the sort order is assumed to be ascending, which is the default sort specification. The next query displays the titles of employees in ascending (alphabetical) order and within that displays the salaries of the employees with the same title in descending order:

```
02:     select     E.eTitle, E.eSalary
        from       employee E
        order by   E.eTitle asc, E.eSalary desc;
```

The specification of the attributes in the `order by` clause may use a position reference instead of an attribute name:

```
03:     select     E.eTitle, E.eSalary
        from       employee E
        order by   1 asc, 2 desc;
```

Although SQL allows this by-position syntax specification for the `order by` clause, the by-name syntax is more readable. Since SQL allows for the selective renaming of a column in the select clause, the by-name syntax is preferred.

As indicated, the `order by` clause sorts the tuples in the result of a query. The `order by` clause cannot be used in an arbitrary table expression. Tables in SQL are still unordered collections of tuples. Therefore, the `order by` clause can not be used in a view definition since views are virtual tables.

5.4.3 Aggregation

Many important queries over the data in a database involve aggregation of results, such as queries involving minimum, maximum, sum, count, and average. The formal query languages of relational algebra and relational calculus do not provide inherent support for aggregation, although queries involving minimum or maximum and a limited form of counting (more than one or only one) can be expressed in these languages, as illustrated in the earlier chapters. However, SQL provides inherent support in the language for aggregation constructs.

Consider the following query that finds the minimum, maximum and average employee salary, as well as the sum of all salaries and a count of the number of employees in the database:

```
√A1:    select  min(E.eSalary), max(E.eSalary),
                avg(E.eSalary), sum(E.eSalary), count(*)
        from    employee E;
```

This query returns a single tuple with five attribute values. The `min`, `max`, `avg` and `sum` aggregate functions apply to a numeric attribute. The `count(*)` counts the number of tuples in the result of the `from` clause, since there is no `where` clause specified.

As another example, consider a query that counts the number of employees that took a training course in the database technology area:

```
√A2:    select  count(distinct T.eID)
        from    dbCourse D, takes T
        where   D.cID = T.cID;
```

Since an employee can take many training courses in the database technology area, the count aggregate function counts the number of `distinct` employee IDs.

Grouping. In the previous example, the aggregation applied to all of the tuples in the result of the (`from` and) `where` clause. Some queries require applying an aggregate function to groups of tuples that have the same value on a grouping of attributes. SQL provides a `group by` clause for the specification of the grouping attributes. For example, consider the query that finds the minimum, maximum, and average salary of employees by title:

```
√G1:    select    E.eTitle, min(E.eSalary),
                  max(E.eSalary), avg(E.eSalary)
        from      employee E
        group by  E.eTitle;
```

The database system groups together the tuples that have the same value of `eTitle` and finds the minimum, maximum, and average `eSalary` of the employees in each group.

As another example, for each technology area, find the number of employees that took training courses in that technology area. Display the identification number of the technology area, its title, and the number of employees:

```
√G2:    select    A.aID, A.aTitle,
                  count(distinct T.eID) as numEmps
        from      technologyArea A, trainingCourse C, takes T
        where     A.aID = C.areaID and
                  C.cID = T.cID
        group by  A.aID, A.aTitle;
```

Notice that the group by clause specifies both the aID and aTitle attributes. If only the aID attribute is specified in the group by clause while both the aID and aTitle attributes are specified in the select clause, SQL does not know what to do if more than one value of aTitle occurs in combination with an aID value. Therefore, SQL requires that any nonaggregate columns appearing in the select clause appear in the group by clause, so that the aggregates produce a single result for each group.

Having. SQL also supports the ability to place a selection condition on the results of grouping by the having clause. For example, consider a modification of the query G2 that identifies technology areas with at least 4 employees that took training courses in that technology area and displays the result in descending order on the number of employees:

```
H1:     select      A.aID, A.aTitle,
                    count(distinct T.eID) as numEmps
        from        technologyArea A, trainingCourse C, takes T
        where       A.aID = C.areaID and
                    C.cID = T.cID
        group by    A.aID, A.aTitle
        having      numEmps >= 4
        order by    numEmps desc;
```

The having clause avoids a two-step process. Assume that the query G2 is the defining expression for a view named numEmpsTakenArea; then the following query generates the same results as query H1:

```
√H2:    select      *
        from        numEmpsTakenArea
        where       numEmps >= 4
        order by    numEmps desc;
```

The query Q4 that finds the employees who took courses in more than one technology area can also be rephrased using aggregation, grouping, and having. Query Q4A*i* defines a view moreThanOneTechArea that finds the employees who took courses in more than one technology area:

```
Q4Ai:   create      view moreThanOneTechArea as
        select      T.eID, count(distinct areaID) as numAreas
        from        takes T, trainingCourse C
        where       T.cID = C.cID
        group by    T.eID
        having      numAreas > 1;
```

Query Q4A*ii* joins the view defined in Q4A*i* with the `employee` table to return the desired attributes:

```
Q4Aii:   select  E.eID, E.eLast, E.eFirst, E.eTitle
         from    employee E
         where   exists
                 (select *
                 from     moreThanOneTechArea M
                 where    M.eID=E.eID);
```

5.4.4 Nested Subqueries

Earlier in the chapter, the `exists` and `not exists` subqueries illustrated nested subqueries and the use of existential conditions in the `where` clause to support division and to optionally support the specification of difference and intersection. Nested subqueries also provide a mechanism to support equality and set comparisons.

Equality Comparison. Consider another specification of Q1 that finds the courses in the database technology area:

```
√Q1A:     create view dbCourse as
          select C.cID, C.cTitle, C.cHours
          from   trainingCourse C
          where  C.areaID =
                 (select   A.aID
                 from      technologyArea A
                 where     A.aTitle = 'Database');
```

The conditional expression in the `where` clause allows for an equality comparison between the `areaID` attribute of the `trainingCourse` table and the result of a `select–from–where` expression that returns the identification number of the database technology area.

There are constraints on the use of the equality comparison. The nested subquery must return a single tuple, and the items being compared must be compatible. In Q1A, the nested subquery retrieves the key of the `technologyArea` table, and it is compared to its referencing foreign key in the `trainingCourse` table.

The nested subquery of Q1A is not a correlated subquery. The nested subquery is executed once to find the identification number of the database technology area, which is then compared with the `areaID` attribute of a `trainingCourse`. The earlier existential examples presented were nested correlated subqueries where the table aliases in the outer query are referenced in the subquery. Thus, the correlated subquery is evaluated for each value in the outer query.

Besides being used to compare a foreign key with the primary key that it references, equality comparisons are useful in the presence of aggregation. Query Q5 retrieved the employee information for those employees having the minimum salary: finding those employees where it is not the case that there exists another employee that has a smaller salary.

Consider another specification of this query using the inherent aggregation capabilities of SQL to find the employees whose salary is equal to the minimum employee salary.

```
√Q5A:   select  E.eID, E.eLast, E.eFirst, E.eTitle
        from    employee E
        where   E.eSalary =
                (select min(S.eSalary)
                from    employee S );
```

The nested subquery of Q5A is not correlated, since it finds the minimum salary once, which is compared with an employee's salary in the conditional expression of the `where` clause.

Set Comparison. The conditional expression in the `where` clause also allows for the specification of comparisons based on set membership using the `in` and `not in` operators. Some of the example nested correlated subqueries can be rewritten to noncorrelated nested subqueries using set comparisons.

For example, query Q2 finds those employees who have taken a training course in the database technology area. Query Q2A answers the same query by retrieving the requested employee information for those employees whose `eID` value appears in the multiset of employee IDs who have taken a course in the database technology area:

```
√Q2A:   select  E.eID, E.eLast, E.eFirst, E.eTitle
        from    employee E
        where   E.eID in
                (select T.eID
                from    takes T, dbCourse D
                where   T.cID=D.cID);
```

As another example, query Q3 finds those employees that have not taken any training courses. Query Q3A answers the same query by retrieving the requested employee information for those employees whose `eID` value does *not* appear in the multiset of employee IDs that have taken any training course:

```
√Q3A:   select  E.eID, E.eLast, E.eFirst, E.eTitle
        from    employee E
        where   E.eID not in
```

```
    (select T.eID
    from   takes T);
```

Both of the preceding examples replace a nested correlated subquery using an existential comparison with a nested uncorrelated subquery using a set comparison. The nested correlated subquery is executed once for each value in the outer query, whereas the nested uncorrelated subquery is executed once, and each value in the outer query is checked for membership in the resulting multiset.

5.4.5 Joined Tables

Recall the query Q1 that finds the training courses offered in the database technology area. The original specification of Q1 followed the TRC specification of the query using an existential condition in the `where` clause. The query Q1A specified the same query using the `in` set comparison operator in the `where` clause. The query can also be specified using join conditions in the `where` clause. In query Q1B, the `trainingCourse` and the `technologyArea` tables are joined by the condition `C.areaID = A.aID` in the `where` clause:

```
√Q1B:  create view dbCourse as
       select C.cID, C.cTitle, C.cHours
       from   trainingCourse C, technologyArea A
       where  C.areaID = A.aID and A.aTitle = 'Database';
```

One of the most common mistakes in forming a query expression in SQL is omitting of the join conditions in the `where` clause of the query. In the foregoing example, if the join condition (`C.areaID = A.aID`) is omitted, then the result contains the database technology area combined in a cartesian product with all of the rows in the `trainingCourse` table.

The SQL-92 revision of the standard introduced *joined tables* to allow the specification of a join in the `from` clause of an SQL query. In the Q1C specification of the query, the `trainingCourse` and `technologyArea` tables are explicitly joined in the `from` clause on their related attributes rather than the implicit join of Q1B specified in the `where` clause:

```
Q1C:   create view dbCourse as
       select C.cID, C.cTitle, C.cHours
       from   (trainingCourse C join technologyArea A
              on areaID=aID)
       where  A.aTitle = 'Database';
```

This revision of the standard also allowed for a *natural join* specification in the `from` clause. A natural join is a shorthand specification of an equality join, where the attributes having the same name in both tables are joined such that they are equal and only one copy of the attribute is included in the result. Recall query Q2, which finds those employees who have taken a training course in the database technology area. The query Q2A specified the same query using the `in` set membership comparison operator in the `where` clause. The query can also be specified using natural joined tables in the `from` clause. Query Q2B answers the same query by performing a natural join of the `employee`, `takes` and `dbCourse` tables. The `takes` and `dbCourse` tables are natural joined on the `cID` attribute and the result is natural joined with the `employee` table on the `eID` attribute:

```
Q2B:    select  distinct E.eID, E.eLast, E.eFirst, E.eTitle
        from    (employee E natural join
                (takes T natural join dbCourse D));
```

Obviously, the natural join is based on the attributes having the same name. The `as` construct allows for the renaming of tables and attributes in the `from` clause to facilitate a natural join instead of an explicit join. Query Q1D renames the `technologyArea` table to the `area` table with its `aID` attribute renamed to `areaID` to perform a natural join:

```
Q1D:    create view dbCourse as
        select cID, cTitle, cHours
        from   (trainingCourse natural join
               (technologyArea as
               area(areaID, aTitle, aURL, aLeadID)))
        where  aTitle = 'Database';
```

All of the basic SQL queries with the joined conditions specified in the `where` clause are still valid SQL queries. The joined tables capability provides an alternative specification of the query.

5.5 QUERY OPTIMIZATION

In the procedural relational algebra language, the concept of query optimization was introduced to motivate that alternative query specifications may result in varying performance. Heuristics were discussed to perform selections as early as possible and to reorder joins using the theoretical properties of the relational operators to find an alternative specification of the query that was more efficient. Query optimization is also important in declarative languages, although the coverage of the declarative query languages (DRC, TRC, and SQL) thus far has emphasized the correct specification of a query. After all, the declarative query languages specify what data to retrieve and not how to retrieve the data. However, it is this declarative specification of *what* data to retrieve instead of *how* to retrieve the data that leads to the concept of query optimization for SQL.

There are obviously different ways to specify the characteristics of the data to be retrieved in SQL, and these alternative query specifications may result in query executions with different performance characteristics. A review of the various specifications for the query Q2, which finds the employees who took a training course offered in the database technology area, illustrates some of the differences in the query evaluation.

The original specification of Q2 uses a nested correlated subquery to illustrate the `exists` conditional and the similarity of SQL to TRC:

```
√Q2:    select  E.eID, E.eLast, E.eFirst, E.eTitle
        from    employee E
        where   exists
                (select *
                from    takes T, dbCourse D
                where   T.eID=E.eID and T.cID=D.cID);
```

Since the inner query is correlated on the employee `eID`, the nested query must be executed for each employee tuple.

The Q2A specification uses a nested uncorrelated query to illustrate the use of the `in` set membership conditional:

```
√Q2A:   select  E.eID, E.eLast, E.eFirst, E.eTitle
        from    employee E
        where   E.eID in
                (select T.eID
                from    takes T, dbCourse D
                where   T.cID=D.cID);
```

Since the nested query is not correlated, the subquery can be evaluated once, but each employee ID value is checked for membership in the result of the inner query.

The Q2B specification illustrates the natural join option in the `from` clause:

```
Q2B:    select  distinct E.eID, E.eLast, E.eFirst, E.eTitle
        from    (employee E natural join
                (takes T natural join dbCourse D));
```

which is the variation of another specification of the query Q2C that incorporates the join conditions in the `where` clause:

```
√Q2C:   select  distinct E.eID, E.eLast, E.eFirst, E.eTitle
        from    employee E, takes T, dbCourse D
        where   E.eID = T.eID and T.cID=D.cID;
```

Both of these unnested versions of Q2 require the removal of duplicates using `distinct`, since an employee can be included in the result for each database training course the employee took.

To summarize, some of the alternatives for specifying query Q2 include

- nested correlated subquery using an existential conditional
- nested uncorrelated subquery using the set membership comparison
- unnested query with joined tables in the `from` clause requiring distinct to remove duplicates.
- unnested query with join specified in the `where` clause requiring distinct to remove duplicates

In general terms, an unnested version of a query is usually more efficient than a nested version. Similarly, a nested uncorrelated specification is generally evaluated more efficiently than a correlated one. Also, using joined tables in the `from` clause may be evaluated more efficiently than a corresponding join specified in the `where` clause.

Although query optimization is the responsibility of the database system, the performance of the database application is ultimately the responsibility of the database administrator (DBA). If the performance of certain queries is not appropriate, the DBA is responsible for tuning the database, based on guidelines for database administration provided in the manual for the particular database product employed in the application. Obviously, adding indexes to certain attributes or combination of attributes may improve performance. However, revising the specification of a query may also be necessary. Most database products provide the ability to view the plan for evaluating a query, which can be used in conjunction with vendor guidelines to tune the performance of the database application.

5.6 BEYOND THE QUERY LANGUAGE

Although SQL is short for Structured Query Language, the SQL standard has evolved to include a DDL for defining tables and relationships between tables; a DML for inserting, updating, and deleting tuples from tables; and a DCL for database integrity and security.

5.6.1 Data Definition Language

A DDL is a language used for defining the database. The data definition component of SQL was added to the standard in SQL-92. The following defines the `technologyArea` table in SQL:

```
create table technologyArea
(   aID     char(3)     not null,
    aTitle  varchar(20) not null,
    aURL    varchar(50) default
                        'http://www.company.intranet/technology/',
    aLeadID char(9)     not null,
    constraint areaKey
            primary key (aID),
    constraint areaUniqueTitle
            unique (aTitle),
    constraint areaUniqueLead
            unique (aLeadID),
    constraint areaForeignKey
            foreign key (aLeadID) references employee (eID)
            on update cascade;);
```

The name and data type or domain of each attribute of the table is declared along with any constraints for that attribute. The standard supports scalar data types that include fixed- and varying-length character string data types, fixed- and varying-length bit string data types, and various types for numbers, including `smallint`, `integer`, `decimal`, and `float`. Possible attribute constraints include `not null` and `default` value. The `not null` constraint indicates that a `null` value is not permitted for that attribute. The `default` value constraint uses the default value specified for that attribute when an explicit value is not given when creating a new tuple. In the `technologyArea` table, the URL for the company's main technology Web page is given as the default value for the `aURL` attribute.

The definition of table constraints follows the attribute definitions. Possible table constraints include a primary key constraint, uniqueness constraint, and referential integrity. For the `technologyArea` table, the attribute `aID` forms the primary key, the attributes `aTitle` and `aLeadID` must be unique, and the attribute `aLeadID` is a foreign key that references the primary key `eID` of the `employee` table. Each of these table constraints can be optionally named as shown to allow for explicit deletion if desired. The referential integrity constraint allows for the specification of actions for a delete or an update of the referenced attribute. Since there is no action specified for delete, the database system will not allow the removal of an employee whose identification number is the value of the `aLeadID` attribute for some tuple in the `technologyArea` table. The action specified for an update of the `eID` attribute of the `employee` table that appears as a foreign key in the `technologyArea` table is to automatically `cascade` this update to the foreign key `aLeadID`. Other referential triggered actions include `set default` to automatically set the foreign key value to a default value for the attribute and `set null` to automatically set the foreign key value to a null value. The action specified depends on the semantics of the enterprise and must be wisely chosen by the database designer.

5.6.2 Data Manipulation Language

DML extends the query language with the capability to insert, update, and delete tuples from tables.

The `insert` statement provides the ability to insert data into a table. The following example illustrates an insert using explicit values to add a row to the `employee` table:

```
I1:     insert into employee values
        ('111', 'Last111', 'First111', 'Data Administrator', 75111);
```

In the example `I1`, the columns of `employee` are assumed to be in a left-to-right ordering of the fields of the table. However, the insert statement also allows an optional attribute list to specify a different ordering of attributes or to take advantage of the specification of default values. Recall that the `create table` statement for `technologyArea` defined a default value for the URL: `'http://www.company.intranet/technology/'`. The following `insert` statement adds a new `technologyArea` tuple for the `'Web'` technology area. Since the `aURL` attribute is not included in the list, the default value for the URL is used:

```
I2:     insert  into technologyArea (aID, aTitle, aLeadID)
        values  ('WW', 'Web', '369');
```

A select statement can also be used as the source of an insert into statement. Assuming that the table `managers` has been defined appropriately by a create table statement, then the `managers` table can be populated with the identification number of employees having the title '`Manager`':

```
I3:     insert  into managers
        select  eID
        from    employee
        where   eTitle = 'Manager';
```

In this case, `managers` is an intermediate table, which is populated at the time that the insert statement is executed.

The `update` statement provides the ability to change existing data in a table. The following example illustrates an update that gives employees who lead technology areas a 3% raise:

```
U1:     update  employee
        set     eSalary = eSalary * 1.03
        where   E.eID in
                (select A.aLeadID
                from    technologyArea A);
```

The set clause specifies the attribute and its modified value. In the preceding example, the eSalary attribute is increased by 3%. If additional attributes are to be changed, a comma is used to separate the update specification for each attribute. The where clause specifies the rows of the table to be updated. If all rows are to be modified, then the where clause is not specified. In the example, the where clause restricts the update of the salary to only those employees who lead technology areas.

The delete statement provides the ability to delete data from a table. The following example illustrates the deletion of technology areas that do not offer any training courses:

```
D1:     delete from technologyArea
        where       aID not in
                    (select C.areaID
                    from    trainingCourse C);
```

The where clause restricts the delete operation to the rows that satisfy the where condition. If the where clause is not specified, then all rows of the table are removed. In the foregoing example, the where clause specifies that rows in the technologyArea table will be deleted if the aID attribute value does not appear as an areaID value in any trainingCourse row.

5.6.3 Data Control

SQL also includes components for data control: integrity and security. Both integrity and security are important components of a database system. SQL allows for the specification of general integrity constraints that validate the data in the database for consistency. It also supports the granting and revoking of access privileges for data security.

Integrity. The data integrity component of a database system maintains the correctness of the data according to the semantics of the enterprise as specified in the database implementation. Some common integrity constraint specifications are built in to the DDL, such as attribute and table constraints. Most of these constraints are a shorthand for common integrity constraints that can be specified using an integrity constraint specification language.

SQL provides a create assertion statement for the specification of general integrity constraints, which specifies a check condition that must be TRUE for every database instance. In the following example of a general integrity constraint, assume that an employee lead must have taken at least one course in the technology area that they lead:

```
create  assertion areaLeadAtLeastOne
check   (not exists
            (select *
```

```
from        technologyArea A
where       A.aLeadID not in
    (select T.eID
    from    takes T, trainingCourse C
    where   T.cID = C.cID and
            C.areaID=A.aID)));
```

The constraint is violated if the check condition evaluates to FALSE. In this example, the condition is violated if there exists a tuple in the technologyArea table where the value of the aLeadID value does not appear in the multiset of employee IDs that have taken a course in that technology area.

Security. The security component of a database system is responsible for enforcing the access rules, based on the discretionary privileges granted on a database object. SQL incorporates table privileges that are granted to or revoked from an authorized database user on a table. The owner of the database table is the authorized database user who created the table. The table owner is automatically granted all table privileges on the created table. The owner of the table may then use the grant and revoke statements to manage the privileges on the database table.

The table privileges include select, insert, update, delete, and reference. An authorized database user must have the select table privilege to access any column of a table. Inserting data into a table requires the insert table privilege, which can be restricted to specify a list of named columns. Similarly, the update privilege allows a user to update data in a table, and this privilege can be restricted to specify the columns of the table that the authorized user is allowed to update. An authorized database user must have the delete table privilege to delete any tuples from a table. The reference table privilege, which may be restricted to columns of a table, allows the column of a table to be referenced in the specification of an integrity constraint.

The grant statement adds the list of privileges on the given tables to the list of users specified. Assume that there is a training department that is responsible for the technical training courses and enrollment for those courses within the company. The training department can grant the select privilege to humanResources on the takes, trainingCourse, and technologyArea tables, so that the humanResources user can determine the skill set of an employee:

```
grant   select
on      takes, trainingCourse, technologyArea
to      humanResources
```

When granting privileges, the user granting the privileges may optionally specify the with grant option, which allows the users to grant these privileges (or a subset thereof) to other authorized database users. Assume that humanResources is the owner of the employee table. The humanResources user must grant the reference privilege on the eID attribute of the employee table to the trainingCoordinator so that the employee identification number entered in the takes table can be verified for referential integrity. The with grant option allows the trainingCoordinator to grant this reference privilege to another authorized database user.

```
grant   reference(eID)
on      employee
to      trainingCoordinator
with grant option
```

The revoke statement removes the list of privileges on the given tables from the list of users specified. In the following revoke statement, the training department removes the ability for humanResources to access the takes table:

```
revoke  select
on      takes
from    humanResources
```

Views also provide a mechanism that works in conjunction with privileges for data security. The insert, update, and reference table privileges can be restricted to specify a list of named columns. However, the select table privilege gives the user access to any column of a table. To restrict a user's access to only some of the columns of a table, a view can be defined on that table to project the desired attributes. A grant statement of the select table privilege on the view allows select access to only those columns provided in the view.

5.7 SUMMARY

SQL uses a syntactic variation of TRC to provide a practical and declarative language to query a relational database. This section provides a brief syntax summary of the SQL constructs described in this chapter, including queries, views, data definition, data manipulation (insert, update, and delete), integrity and security. The conventions for the syntax summary use square brackets [. . .] to denote optional items, | to indicate a choice of one of the items specified, and identifiers in SMALL CAPS to denote items that can be replaced by names or further expanded.

The select statement forms the basis of an SQL query, selecting a list of attributes from a list of tables that optionally satisfy a where condition. The optional keyword distinct returns a set of tuples instead of the default multiset of tuples as the result of the query. The optional group by clause allows for the specification of grouping attributes for the application of aggregate functions (e.g., min, max, avg, sum, count) specified in the select clause. An optional having clause allows for the specification of a condition on the result of the grouping. The result of a query can be optionally ordered using the `order by` clause, which specifies the columns to be ordered and the sort order (either ascending or descending):

```
select       [distinct] ATTRIBUTE-LIST
from         TABLE-LIST
[where       WHERE-CONDITION]
[group by    GROUPING-ATTRIBUTES
[having      HAVING-CONDITION]]
[order by    COLUMN-NAME [ asc | desc ], ... ]
```

A view or virtual table provides the inherent capability for abstraction, associating the name of the view with a defining select statement, which is executed each time the view name is referenced:

```
create view VIEW-NAME as
SELECT-STATEMENT
```

SQL also includes a DDL that provides the capability to define tables. Each attribute or column is defined to be of a specified type and can have associated attribute constraints, such as `not null` or `default` value. The list of table constraints include primary key, uniqueness, and referential integrity (foreign key) constraints:

```
create table TABLE-NAME
(
COLUMN-NAME     COLUMN-TYPE        [ATTRIBUTE-CONSTRAINT],
                ...
[ TABLE-CONSTRAINT-LIST ]
)
```

SQL also provides statements for data manipulation, including `insert`, `update`, and `delete`:

The `insert into` statement provides a mechanism to insert tuples into the named table according to the specified ATTRIBUTE-LIST using the specified SOURCE:

```
insert into TABLE-NAME [ (ATTRIBUTE-LIST) ]
SOURCE
```

The SOURCE of the `insert into` statement is either a list of explicit values, as in

```
insert into TABLE-NAME [ (ATTRIBUTE-LIST) ]
values ( EXPLICIT-VALUES )
```

or the specification of a select statement, as in

```
insert into TABLE-NAME [ (ATTRIBUTE-LIST) ]
SELECT-STATEMENT
```

In either case, if a column of TABLE-NAME is not included in the ATTRIBUTE-LIST, then a default value is assigned for that column. Note that if an omitted column does not have a default value specified in the DDL for TABLE-NAME, then the insert results in an error. If ATTRIBUTE-LIST is not specified, then a left-to-right ordering of the attributes within that table is assumed.

The `update` statement modifies the columns given in the `set` clause to the values determined by the expressions specified. The optional `where` clause can restrict the rows of the table to be updated:

```
update  TABLE-NAME
set     COLUMN-NAME = VALUE-EXPRESSION, . . .
[where  UPDATE-CONDITION]
```

The `delete` statement removes tuples from the table specified. The optional `where` clause restricts the delete operation to the rows that satisfy the DELETE-CONDITION. If the `where` clause is not specified, then all rows of the table are deleted:

```
delete  from TABLE-NAME
[where  DELETE-CONDITION]
```

Integrity constraints validate the data in the database. SQL provides for the specification of general integrity constraints with the `create assertion` statement, which checks that the ASSERTION-CONDITION specified is TRUE on every database instance:

```
create  assertion ASSERTION-NAME
check   (ASSERTION-CONDITION)
```

The security component of SQL incorporates table privileges that are granted to or revoked from an authorized database user on a table. The table privileges include `select`, `insert`, `update`, `delete`, and `reference`. The `grant` statement adds the list of privileges on the given tables to the list of users specified. When granting privileges, the user granting the privileges may optionally specify the `with grant option`, which allows the users in the USER-LIST to grant these privileges (or a subset thereof) to other authorized database users:

```
grant   PRIVILEGE-LIST
on      TABLE-COLUMN-LIST
to      USER-LIST
[with grant option]
```

The `revoke` statement removes the list of privileges on the given tables from the list of users specified:

```
revoke  PRIVILEGE-LIST
on      TABLE-COLUMN-LIST
from    USER-LIST
```

EXERCISES

√ Use the educational tool to *check* the answers to these queries.

√**5.1** Answer the following queries in SQL over the EMPLOYEE TRAINING schema:

```
employee(eID, eLast, eFirst, eTitle, eSalary)
technologyArea(aID, aTitle, aURL, aLeadID)
trainingCourse(cID, cTitle, cHours, areaID)
takes(eID, cID, tYear, tMonth, tDay)
```

(a) Which employees took the 'Enterprise JavaBeans' training course?

`(eID, eLast, eFirst, eTitle)`

(b) Which coaches have not taken a training course in the 'Java' technology area?

`(eID, eLast, eFirst)`

(c) Which employees took *more than one* course in the 'Database' technology area?

`(eID, eLast, eFirst, eTitle)`

(d) Who is the lowest-paid manager?

`(eID, eLast, eFirst, eTitle, eSalary)`

(e) What are the titles of employees who earn more than a 'Coach'?

`(eTitle)`

(f) Which leads have taken *all* of the training courses in the technology area that they lead?

`(eID, eLast, eFirst, eTitle)`

(g) What is the schedule of training courses? Display the results in chronological order within an ascending order on technology area and training course:

`(aID, aTitle, cID, cTitle, tYear, tMonth, tDay)`

(h) For each employee that has taken a training course in a technology area, compute the total number of hours taken in that technology area:

`(eID, eLast, eFirst, aID, aTitle, totalHours)`

(i) For each training course that has been taken by at least four employees, compute the total number of employees that have taken that course:

`(cID, cTitle, totalEmps)`

(j) For each technology area that offers a training course, compute the total number of hours of training offered in that technology area. Display the results in descending order on the number of hours:

`(aID, aTitle, numberOfHours)`

√**5.2** Answer Exercise 4.1 in SQL. Do not translate the TRC solutions to SQL! Verify that you obtained the same set of results on the same database instance for each query.

√**5.3** Answer Exercise 3.1 in SQL. Verify your results, and compare your solutions.

√**5.4** Answer Exercise 2.1 in SQL. Verify your results, and compare your solutions.

5.5 Data validation is an important feature of database systems. The DDL of SQL allows for the inherent specification of constraints in the `create table` statement that would otherwise need to be specified using an explicit constraint language. For the following constraints over the EMPLOYEE TRAINING schema, write explicit integrity constraints in SQL to verify the data in the database (you may assume that there are no null values in the database instance):

(a) Primary Key Constraint
Choose one of the tables from the EMPLOYEE TRAINING database schema, and write an integrity constraint in SQL to verify the primary key constraint.

(b) Referential Integrity Constraint
Choose one of the referential integrity constraints in the EMPLOYEE TRAINING database schema, and write an integrity constraint in SQL to verify the referential integrity constraint.

(c) Uniqueness Constraint
Choose one of the tables from the EMPLOYEE TRAINING database schema, and write an integrity constraint in SQL to verify the uniqueness constraint.

5.6 The chapter provided a definition of the `technologyArea` table in SQL. Write the DDL in SQL to define the `takes` and `trainingCourse` tables.

5.7 Write the following data manipulation operations in SQL over the EMPLOYEE TRAINING schema:

(a) Add a new technology area for 'Mobile Computing'.

(b) Modify the lead for the 'Database' technology area.

(c) Remove the training courses that are not taken by any employees.

5.8 Write the following operations in SQL over the EMPLOYEE TRAINING schema:

(a) Allow the 'Human Resources' department to schedule employees for training courses.

(b) Remove the capability of the 'Training Coordinator' to reference the employee table.

POSTSCRIPT

After answering Exercise 5.1 in SQL, you should answer the queries given by 5.1 (a) through (f) in relational algebra, DRC, and TRC. Verify your results, and compare your solutions.

Chapter 6

Case Studies

Up to this point, the four query languages (relational algebra, DRC, TRC, and SQL) have been explored each in its own chapter in the context of only the EMPLOYEE TRAINING enterprise. This chapter presents three case studies: WEB PAGE, NEW HOME, and INVESTMENT PORTFOLIO. Each enterprise is defined by a high-level description of its requirements, which is then mapped into its conceptual design as an ER diagram. The ER diagram is then mapped into a corresponding relational schema. Ten queries over each enterprise illustrating various types of queries are used to provide a side-by-side comparison of the four query languages[1].

6.1 WEB PAGE

The WEB PAGE case study is based on a database for Web pages, specifically for maintaining a Web site related to courses taught at a university. Each course has an associated Web site for maintaining all of the course material, including class notes, associated publications, sample documents, executable files, and database files. This courseware is stored in a particular directory on the Web site, and access is provided by means of a file transfer protocol used for transferring files between computers. The graphics associated with a Web page are also stored in a directory, and the database records the display of a graphic by a Web page. Obviously, Web pages are linked to other Web pages by hypertext transfer protocol links. Each Web page is associated with the main Web page for a course, which is called its *base*.

[1]For each enterprise, a database instance and the 10 queries specified in each language are available at this book's companion website.

Conceptual Design

Based on the high-level introduction to the WEB PAGE enterprise, assume the following:

- The characteristics of a Web page include a unique identification number, a title, its Uniform Resource Locator (URL), which gives the address of the Web page, and the number of times that the Web page has been accessed, or hits. A course Web page has an associated *base* page and a base Web page serves as the base of all of the Web pages associated with the course.
- The characteristics of a graphic include a unique identification number, the name of the graphic, the format of the image, such as 'gif', 'jpg' or 'bmp', and the directory in which the graphic image is located. A graphic can be displayed by many Web pages, and a Web page can display many graphics.
- The characteristics of courseware include a unique identification number, a description of the course material, the directory in which the material is located and a category describing the type of course material, such as 'P' for publication, 'N' for notes, 'D' for sample documents, 'E' for executable files and 'M' for database files. A courseware file can be linked to by several Web pages and a Web page can provide ftp links to several courseware files.

The conceptual design for the WEB PAGE enterprise is given by the ER diagram of Figure 6.1. The entities and the relationships of the WEB PAGE enterprise

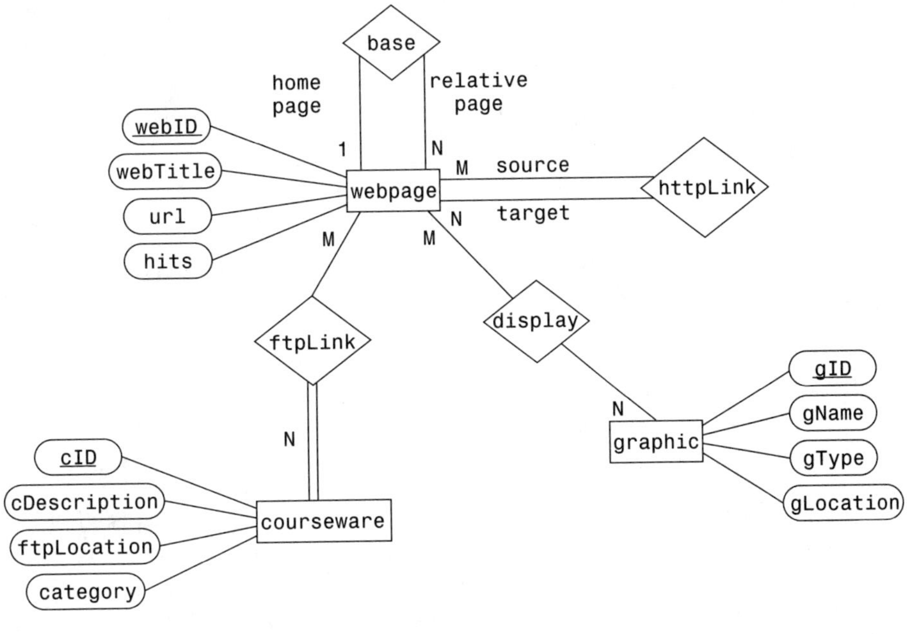

Figure 6.1 WEB PAGE ER diagram.

TABLE 6.1 Web Page entity summary.

Entity	Attribute	Type	Description
webpage	webID	C	The unique ID that identifies a Web page.
	webTitle	C	The title of the Web page.
	url	C	The URL of the Web page.
	hits	N	The number of hits to the Web page.
graphic	gID	C	The unique id to identify an image.
	gName	C	The name of the image.
	gType	C	The format in which the image is saved:'gif', 'jpg', or 'bmp'.
	gLocation	C	The directory in which the image is located.
courseware	cID	C	The unique id to identify a courseware file.
	cDescription	C	The description of the courseware file.
	ftpLocation	C	The directory where the file can be ftped.
	category	C	The category of courseware: 'P' = publication, 'N' = notes, 'D' = document, 'E' = executable, 'M' = mdb file.

TABLE 6.2 Web Page relationship summary.

Relationship	Description
ftpLink	A M: N relationship between a web page and courseware. One Web page can have ftp links to multiple courseware files, and one courseware file can be linked to by different Web pages.
display	A M: N relationship between a Web page and graphics. One page can display multiple images, and the same image can be displayed on several pages.
base	A 1: N recursive relationship between web pages. Every Web page can have just one base Web page, but a base page can be the base of many Web pages.
httpLink	A M: N recursive relationship between Web pages. One Web page can have links to multiple Web pages, and each page can be linked from different pages.

are summarized in Table 6.1 and Table 6.2, respectively. Table 6.1 includes a `Type` attribute that indicates whether the attribute is of type character string (C) or numeric (N). The ER diagram contains two recursive relationships (`base` and `httpLink`). Role names on the edges linking the relationship to the entity indicate the role that the entity plays with respect to the cardinality ratio of the relationship. For example, one Web page that is the home page for the course Web site has many relative Web pages that make up the web site, and a relative page within the web site has one `base` Web page. As another example, a Web page can be the source and target of many `httpLinks`.

RELATIONAL SCHEMA

The mapping of the conceptual design of the WEB PAGE enterprise given by Figure 6.1 to a relational schema is shown in Figure 6.2. There is a table for each entity (`webpage, graphic, and courseware`) and for each M:N relationship (`httpLink, display, and ftpLink`) in the ER diagram. The one 1:N relationship `base` is mapped as the `base` attribute of the `webpage` table, since a Web page has exactly one base Web page. In the `httpLink` table, the role names on the edges of the corresponding relationship are used to form the attribute names `sourceWebID` and `targetWebID`.

```
webpage (webID, web Title, url, base, hits)
httpLink (sourceWebID, targetWebID)
graphic (gID, gName, gType, gLocation)
display (webID, gID)
courseware (cID, cDescription, ftpLocation, category)
ftpLink (webID, cID)
```

Figure 6.2 WEB PAGE relational schema.

Queries

The queries of Table 6.3 over the WEB PAGE database schema illustrate various types of database queries in a side-by-side comparison of the query languages. The complex aggregation queries of 9 and 10 can only be answered in SQL, whereas queries 1 through 8 are expressible in all four query languages. The sample query solutions that follow illustrate one possible answer to each query. Other solutions are possible, which should be evident by earlier discussions on query optimization. Since relational algebra query specifications can be disconcerting, these sample relational algebra solutions are designed to break down the answers into reasonable steps using intermediate tables with descriptive names.

√Q1.1: Which pages contain (ftp links to) the class notes?

`(webID, webTitle, url, base)`

Relational Algebra

$\texttt{notesCIDs} := \pi_{\texttt{cID}}\ (\sigma_{\texttt{category='N'}}\ (\texttt{courseware}));$
$\texttt{notesWebIDs} := \pi_{\texttt{webID}}\ (\texttt{notesCIDs} \bowtie \texttt{ftpLink});$
$\pi_{\texttt{webID,webTitle,url,base}}\ (\texttt{webpage} \bowtie \texttt{notesWebIDs});$

TABLE 6.3 WEB PAGE query summary.

Query	Query Description
Q1.1	Which pages contain (ftp links to) the class notes?
Q1.2	Which pages display graphics having the name 'asulogo'?
Q1.3	Which pages do not display any graphics?
Q1.4	Which pages use 'gif' graphics but not 'jpg' graphics?
Q1.5	Which pages contain more than one (ftp) link to courseware?
Q1.6	Which pages contain only one (http) link to another Web page?
Q1.7	Which pages have the most hits?
Q1.8	Which pages contain (ftp) links to all courseware in the publications category?
Q1.9	For each Web page and graphic type, give the number of graphics of that type displayed on that page. Display your results in ascending order on `webID` and, within that, in ascending order on graphic type (`gType`).
Q1.10	For each group of pages belonging to a base, give the average number of hits, the minimum number of hits in that group, the maximum number of hits in that group, and the sum of hits for that group. Display your results in descending order on average number of hits.

DRC

```
{ WebID, WebTitle, URL, Base | (exists CID)
    (courseware(CID, _, _, 'N') and
    ftpLink(WebID, CID) and
    webpage(WebID, WebTitle, URL, Base, _) ) };
```

TRC

```
{ W.webID, W.webTitle, W.url, W.base | (exists C, F)
    (courseware(C) and C.category = 'N' and
    ftpLink(F) and F.cID = C.cID and
    webpage(W) and W.webID = F.webID ) };
```

SQL

```
select   distinct W.webID, W.webTitle, W.url, W.base
from     courseware C, ftpLink F, webpage W
where    C.category = 'N' and F.cID = C.cID and
         W.webID = F.webID;
```

√Q1.2: Which pages display graphics having the name 'asulogo'?

```
(webID, webTitle, url, base)
```

Relational Algebra

asulogoGID := $\pi_{\texttt{gID}}$ ($\sigma_{\text{gName='asulogo'}}$ (graphic));
asulogoWebIDs := $\pi_{\texttt{webID}}$ (asulogoGID $\bowtie$ display);
$\pi_{\texttt{webID,webTitle,url,base}}$ (webpage $\bowtie$ asulogoWebIDs);

DRC

```
{ WebID, WebTitle, URL, Base | (exists GID)
    (graphic(GID,'asulogo',_,_) and
    display(WebID, GID) and
    webpage(WebID, WebTitle, URL, Base,_) ) };
```

TRC

```
{ W.webID, W.webTitle, W.url, W.base | (exists G,D)
    (graphic(G) and G.gName = 'asulogo' and
    display(D) and D.gID = G.gID and
    webpage(W) and W.webID = D.webID) };
```

SQL

```
select  distinct W.webID, W.webTitle, W.url, W.base
from    graphic G, display D, webpage W
where   G.gName = 'asulogo' and D.gID = G.gID and
        W.webID = D.webID;
```

√Q1.3: Which pages do not display any graphics?

(webID, webTitle, url, base)

Relational Algebra

webIDsNoGraphic := ($\pi_{\texttt{webID}}$ (webpage)) − ($\pi_{\texttt{webID}}$ (display));
$\pi_{\texttt{webID,webTitle,url,base}}$ (webpage $\bowtie$ webIDsNoGraphic);

DRC

```
{ WebID, WebTitle, URL, Base |
    webpage(WebID, WebTitle, URL, Base,_) and
    not display(WebID, _) };
```

TRC

```
{ W.webID, W.webTitle, W.url, W.base |
    webpage(W) and not (exists D) (display(D) and
    D.webID = W.webID) };
```

SQL

```
select  W.webID, W.webTitle, W.url, W.base
from    webpage W
where   W.webID not in (select webID from display);
```

√Q1.4: Which pages use 'gif' graphics, but not 'jpg' graphics?

```
(webID, webTitle, url, base)
```

Relational Algebra

gifGIDs := π_{gID} ($\sigma_{\text{gType='gif'}}$ (graphic));
gifWebIDs := π_{webID} (display $\bowtie$ gifGIDs);
jpgGIDs := π_{gID} ($\sigma_{\text{gType='jpg'}}$ (graphic));
jpgWebIDs := π_{webID} (display $\bowtie$ jpgGIDs);
gifNOjpgWebIDs := gifWebIDs − jpgWebIDs;
$\pi_{\text{webID,webTitle,url,base}}$ (webpage $\bowtie$ gifNOjpgWebIDs);

DRC

```
gifWebIDs := { WebID | (exists GID)
    (graphic(GID, _, 'gif', _) and display(WebID, GID) ) };
jpgWebIDs := { WebID | (exists GID)
    (graphic(GID, _, 'jpg', _) and display(WebID, GID) ) };
{ WebID, WebTitle, URL, Base |
    webpage(WebID, WebTitle, URL, Base, _) and
    gifWebIDs(WebID) and not jpgWebIDs(WebID) };
```

TRC

```
gifWebIDs := { D.webID | display(D) and (exists G)
    (graphic(G) and G.gType = 'gif' and G.gID = D.gID) };
jpgWebIDs := { D.webID | display(D) and (exists G)
    (graphic(G) and G.gType = 'jpg' and G.gID = D.gID) };
```

```
{ W.webID, W.webTitle, W.url, W.base |
    webpage(W) and
    (exists G) (gifWebIDs(G) and G.webID = W.webID and
        not (exists J) (jpgWebIDs(J) and
            J.webID = W.webID) ) };
```

SQL

```
gifWebIDs :=
        select  distinct D.webID
        from    display D
        where   exists
                (select *
                from    graphic G
                where   G.gType = 'gif' and G.gID = D.gID) ;

jpgWebIDs :=
        select  distinct D.webID
        from    display D
        where   exists
                (select *
                from    graphic G
                where   G.gType = 'jpg' and G.gID = D.gID) ;

select  W.webID, W.webTitle, W.url, W.base
from    webpage W
where   exists
        (select  *
        from     gifWebIDs G
        where    G.webID = W.webID) and
        not exists
        (select  *
        from     jpgWebIDs J
        where    J.webID = W.webID);
```

√Q1.5: Which pages contain more than one (ftp) link to courseware?

```
(webID, webTitle, url, base)
```

Relational Algebra

ftpLinkCopy (webIDCopy, cIDCopy) := ftpLink;
moreThanOneCourseware :=
    π_{webID} (ftpLink $\bowtie_{webID=webIDCopy \text{ and } cID<>cIDCopy}$ ftpLinkCopy);
$\pi_{webID,webTitle,url,base}$ (webpage $\bowtie$ moreThanOneCourseware);

DRC

```
{WebID, WebTitle, URL, Base | (exists CID)
    (webpage(WebID, WebTitle, URL, Base, _) and
    ftpLink(WebID, CID) and (exists AnotherCID)
    (ftpLink(WebID, AnotherCID) and AnotherCID <> CID)) };
```

TRC

```
{ W.webID, W.webTitle, W.url, W.base |
    webpage (W) and (exists L)
    (ftpLink(L) and L.webID = W.webID and
    (exists F)(ftpLink(F) and F.webID = L.webID and
        F.cID <> L.cID)) };
```

SQL

```
pagesWithMoreThanOneLink(webID, cnt) :=
        select    webID, count(*)
        from      ftpLink
        group by  webID
        having    count(*) > 1;

select    W.webID, W.webTitle, W.url, W.base
from      webpage W, pagesWithMoreThanOneLink P
where     W.webID = P.webID
order by  W.webID asc;
```

√Q1.6: Which pages contain only one (http) link to another Web page?

```
(webID, webTitle, url, base)
```

Relational Algebra

httpLinkCopy (sourceWebIDCopy, targetWebIDCopy) := httpLink;

moreThanOneLink := $\pi_{\text{sourceWebID}}$ (httpLink $\bowtie_{\text{sourceWebID=sourceWebIDCopy and targetWebID<>targetWebIDCopy}}$ httpLinkCopy);

onlyOneLink(webID) := ($\pi_{\text{sourceWebID}}$ (httpLink)) − moreThanOneLink;

$\pi_{\text{webID,webTitle,url,base}}$ (webpage $\bowtie$ onlyOneLink);

DRC

```
{WebID, WebTitle, URL, Base | (exists TargetWebID)
    (webpage(WebID, WebTitle, URL, Base, _) and
    httpLink(WebID, TargetWebID) and
    not (exists AnotherTarget)
        (httpLink(WebID, AnotherTarget) and
        AnotherTarget <> TargetWebID)) };
```

TRC

```
{ W.webID, W.webTitle, W.url, W.base |
   webpage (W) and
   (exists L)(httpLink(L) and L.sourceWebID = W.webID and
       not (exists H)
           (httpLink(H) and
           H.sourceWebID = L.sourceWebID and
           H.targetWebID <> L.targetWebID) ) };
```

SQL

```
pagesWithOneLink (webID, cnt) :=
         select    sourceWebID, count(*)
         from      httpLink
         group by  sourceWebID
         having    count(*) = 1;

select    W.webID, W.webTitle, W.url, W.base
from      webpage W, pagesWithOneLink P
where     W.webID = P.webID
order by  W.webID asc;
```

√Q1.7: Which pages have the most hits?

```
(webID, webTitle, url, base, hits)
```

Relational Algebra

```
webIDsHits := π_webID,hits (webpage);
webIDsHitsCopy (webIDCopy, hitsCopy) := webIDsHits;
webIDsNotMax :=
    π_webID (webIDsHits ⋈_hits<hitsCopy webIDsHitsCopy);
webIDsMaxHits := (π_webID (webpage)) − webIDsNotMax;
webIDsMaxHits ⋈ webpage;
```

DRC

```
{WebID, WebTitle, URL, Base, Hits |
   webpage(WebID, WebTitle, URL, Base, Hits) and
   not (exists H) (webpage(_,_,_,_,H) and H > Hits) };
```

TRC

```
{ W.webID, W.webTitle, W.url, W.base, W.hits |
   webpage(W) and
   not (exists P)(webpage(P) and W.hits < P.hits) };
```

SQL

```
select  *
from    webpage W
where   W.hits = select max(hits) from webpage;
```

√Q1.8: Which pages contain (ftp) links to all courseware in the publications category?

```
(webID, webTitle, url, base)
```

Relational Algebra

pubCIDs := π_{cID} ($\sigma_{category='P'}$ (courseware));
webIDsAllPubs := fttpLink $\div$ pubCIDs;
$\pi_{webID,webTitle,url,base}$ (webpage $\bowtie$ webIDsAllPubs);

DRC

```
pubCIDs := { CID | courseware (CID,_,_,'P') };
{ WebID, WebTitle, URL, Base |
    webpage (WebID, WebTitle, URL, Base, _) and
    (exists C)(pubCIDs(C) and ftpLink(WebID,C)) and
    not (exists CID)(pubCIDs(CID) and
        not ftpLink(WebID, CID) ) };
```

TRC

```
pubCIDs := { C.cID | courseware(C) and C.category = 'P' };
{ W.webID, W.webTitle, W.url, W.base |
    webpage(W) and
```

```
    (exists P,F)(pubCIDs(P) and ftpLink(F) and
        W.webID = F.webID and F.cID = P.cID) and
        not (exists C)(pubCIDs(C) and
            not (exists L)(ftpLink(L) and
                W.webID = L.webID and L.cID = C.cID) ) };
```

SQL

```
pubCIDs :=
        select  *
        from    courseware C
        where   C.category='P';

select  W.webID, W.webTitle, W.url, W.base
from    webpage W
where   exists  (select *
                from    pubCIDs P, ftpLink F
                where   W.webID = F.webID and
                        F.cID = P.cID) and
        not exists
                (select *
                from    pubCIDs C
                where   not exists
                        (select *
                        from    ftpLink L
                        where   L.webID = W.webID and
                                L.cID = C.cID));
```

√Q1.9: For each Web page and graphic type, give the number of graphics of that type displayed on that page. Display your results in ascending order on `webID` and, within that, in ascending order on graphic type (`gType`).

```
(webID, webTitle, url, base, gType, count)
```

SQL

```
gTypeAndCount (webID, gType, cnt) :=
        select   D.webID, G.gType, count(*)
        from     display D, graphic G
        where    D.gID = G.gID
        group by D.webID, G.gType;
```

```
select    W.webID, W.webTitle, W.url, W.base, G.gType, G.cnt
from      webpage W, gTypeAndCount G
where     W.webID = G.webID
order by  W.webID, G.gType;
```

√Q1.10: For each group of pages belonging to a base, give the average number of hits, the minimum number of hits in that group, the maximum number of hits in that group, and the sum of hits for that group. Display your results in descending order on average number of hits:

(webID, webTitle, url, avgHits, minHits, maxHits, sumHits)

SQL

```
aggregates (base, avgHits, minHits, maxHits, sumHits) :=
        select    base, avg (hits), min (hits),
                  max (hits), sum (hits)
        from      webpage
        group by  base;

select    W.webID, W.webTitle, W.url,
          A.avgHits, A.minHits, A.maxHits, A.sumHits
from      webpage W, aggregates A
where     W.webID = A.base
order by  A.avgHits desc;
```

6.2 NEW HOME

The New Home case study maintains information regarding new homebuilders and the models that they offer at various subdivisions. A homebuilder may offer the same model at more than one subdivision, and the price that they offer a model may be different at each subdivision. Each subdivision has lots that are identified by a lot number. Each lot has an associated street address, size in square feet and possibly an additional premium for that lot. A premium is usually assessed if the lot is larger than the average lot or is on a cul de sac or corner within the subdivision. When a lot is sold, there is a homebuilder's model associated with the sale. The status of the sale is also recorded.

CONCEPTUAL DESIGN

Assume the following based on the high-level introduction to the New Home enterprise:

- The characteristics of a homebuilder include a unique identification number, a name, and an address and phone number for the headquarters of that homebuilder. An address is further broken down into the street address, city, and zip code. The state is not recorded in this enterprise, since the state is assumed. A homebuilder offers several models.

- The characteristics of a model include an identification number for the model that is unique for its homebuilder. A model also has a name and square footage. Whether the model is a single story or two story home is also recorded. A model may be offered at various subdivisions. The price that a model is offered at a given subdivision is recorded.
- The characteristics of a subdivision include its name, which is assumed to be unique, and the city and zip code where the subdivision is located. The state is assumed to be local to the enterprise.
- The characteristics of a lot include a lot number that is only unique for its subdivision. Each lot has an associated street address, size in square footage, and a possible premium. A sold lot has a particular homebuilder's model associated with it. The status of the sale indicates whether the house construction is pending or completed.

Figure 6.3 provides an ER diagram capturing the conceptual design of the New Home enterprise. The entities and the relationships of the New Home conceptual design are summarized in Tables 6.4 and 6.5, respectively. The entities `homebuilder`

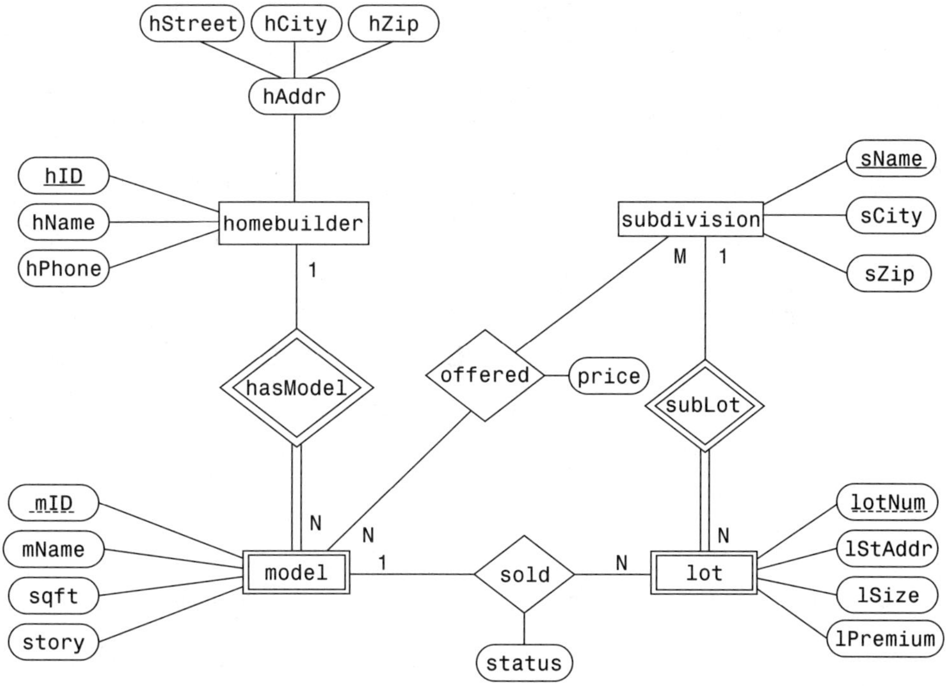

Figure 6.3 New Home ER diagram.

TABLE 6.4 New Home entity summary.

Entity	Attribute	Type	Description
homebuilder	hID	C	The unique ID that identifies a homebuilder.
	hName	C	The name of the homebuilder.
	hPhone	C	The phone number of the homebuilder.
	hStreet	C	The street address of the homebuilder.
	hCity	C	The city of the homebuilder.
	hZip	C	The zip code of the homebuilder.
model	mID	C	The unique ID to identify a model for a homebuilder.
	mName	C	The name of the model.
	sqft	N	The square footage of the model.
	story	C	A '1' or a '2' indicating the number of stories in the model.
subdivision	sName	C	The unique name of the subdivision.
	sCity	C	The city of the subdivision.
	sZip	C	The zip code of the subdivision.
lot	lotNum	C	The unique id to identify a lot within a subdivision.
	lStAddr	C	The street address of the lot.
	lPremium	N	The additional cost associated with the lot.
	lSize	N	The size of a lot in square feet.

TABLE 6.5 New Home relationship summary.

Relationship	Description
offered	An M: N relationship between subdivisions and a model. One subdivision can offer many models, and a model may be offered at many subdivisions. The price attribute, which is a numeric type, represents the price that a homebuilder's model is offered at that subdivision.
hasModel	A 1: N relationship between a homebuilder and a model. A homebuilder has many models, but a model is associated with one homebuilder.
subLot	A 1: N relationship between a subdivision and a lot. A subdivision has many lots but a lot is associated with exactly one subdivision.
sold	A 1: N relationship between a model and a lot. A lot has at most one model that can be on that lot, and a model can be on several lots. The status attribute is of type character string. The status can be either 'P' (pending) or 'C' (closed). A sold lot has a home being built on it of the associated model. A pending status means the house is in the process of being built. A closed status means the house is now completed.

and `subdivision` are strong entities since each have an identification number or name that is unique across the database. The entities `model` and `lot` are weak entities and cannot exist in the database without being associated to a `homebuilder` and `subdivision`, respectively. This existence dependence is modeled in the ER diagram by the total participation of the weak entity in its identifying relationship. Since weak entities cannot be uniquely identified in the database without their associated identifying owner, a model is uniquely identified by a combination of the homebuilder ID and model ID (hID, mID), and a lot is uniquely identified by a combination of the subdivision name and the lot number (sName, lotNum). The price that a model is offered at a subdivision is represented as an attribute of the M:N relationship offered between model and subdivision. The status of a sold lot is an attribute of the 1:N sold relationship between lot and model. Note that the participation constraint of a lot in the sold relationship is partial, since a lot may not be sold.

RELATIONAL SCHEMA

The mapping of the conceptual design of the New Home enterprise given by Figure 6.3 to a relational schema is shown in Figure 6.4. There is a table for each strong entity (homebuilder and subdivision). There is also a table for each weak entity (model and lot), which includes the primary key of its identifying owner. Note that identifying relationships for weak entities are not explicitly mapped to a separate table, but are used to indicate the identifying owner of the weak entity. The remaining relationships (offered and sold) in the ER diagram are each mapped to a table. The offered M:N relationship must be mapped to a separate table, based on the many-to-many characteristics of the relationship. However, the sold 1:N relationship may be mapped either as a separate table or as part of the lot table. If mapped as part of the lot table, then the attributes identifying the model (hID and mID) and the descriptive attribute status would be null for a lot that is available. Since the participation of the lot entity in the sold relationship is partial, the alternative mapping approach of providing a separate table for the sold relationship is appropriate. There is a tuple in the sold table only if the lot is sold. Therefore, a lot is considered available if there is no corresponding tuple in the sold table.

```
homebuilder(hID, hName, hStreet, hCity, hZip, hPhone)
model(hID, mID, mName, sqft, story)
subdivision(sName, sCity, sZip)
offered(sName, hID, mID, price)
lot(sName, lotNum, lStAddr, lSize, lPremium)
sold(sName, lotNum, hID, mID, status)
```

Figure 6.4 New Home relational schema.

QUERIES

This section provides sample queries over the New Home database schema illustrating various types of database queries using all four query languages. A summary of the queries is given in Table 6.6. Queries 9 and 10 require the inherent support of aggregation provided only by SQL.

TABLE 6.6 New Home query summary.

Query	Query Description
Q2.1	Are there subdivisions that only offer single-story homes?
Q2.2	List all the homebuilders who offer single-story models with at least 2000 square feet in subdivisions located in 'Tempe':
Q2.3	Which lots in the 'Terraces' subdivision are available (i.e., not sold)?
Q2.4	Which model(s) are not currently offered in any subdivision?
Q2.5	Which subdivisions offer models from more than one homebuilder?
Q2.6	Which models are offered in only one subdivision?
Q2.7	Which model(s) offered in the 'Foothills' subdivision has the maximum square footage?
Q2.8	Which subdivision offers all the models by the homebuilder 'Homer'?
Q2.9	For each subdivision, find the number of models offered and the average, minimum and maximum price of the models offered at that subdivision. Display the result in descending order on the average price of a home.
Q2.10	For each subdivision, find the total of lot premiums for lots that are available. Display the result in ascending order on the total of lot premiums.

√Q2.1: Are there subdivisions that only offer single-story homes?

```
(sName, sCity, sZip)
```

Relational Algebra

```
subdivisionsOfferSingle :=
     πsName (offered ⋈ (σstory='1' (model) ) );
subdivisionsOfferOther :=
       πsName (offered ⋈ (σstory<>'1' (model) ) );
subdivision ⋈
       (subdivisionsOfferSingle − subdivisionsOfferOther);
```

DRC

```
subdivisionsOfferSingle :=
    {SName |(exists HID, MID)
        (offered(SName, HID, MID, _) and
        model(HID, MID, _, _, '1')) };

subdivisionsOfferOther :=
    {SName |(exists HID, MID, Story)
        (offered(SName, HID, MID, _) and
        model(HID, MID, _, _, Story) and Story<>'1') };

{ SName, SCity, SZip |
    subdivision(SName, SCity, SZip) and
```

```
    subdivisionsOfferSingle(SName) and
    not subdivisionsOfferOther(SName) };
```

TRC

```
subdivisionsOfferSingle :=
    {O.sName |(exists M)
        (offered(O) and model(M) and
        O.hID=M.hID and O.mID=M.mID and M.story = '1') };
subdivisionsOfferOther :=
    {O.sName |(exists M)
        (offered(O) and model(M) and
        O.hID=M.hID and O.mID=M.mID and M.story <> '1') };

{ S | subdivision(S) and
    (exists Single)
        (subdivisionsOfferSingle(Single) and
        S.sName=Single.sName) and
    not (exists Other)
        (subdivisionsOfferOther(Other) and
        S.sName=Other.sName) };
```

SQL

```
subdivisionsOfferSingle :=
        select  distinct O.sName
        from    offered O, model M
        where   O.hID=M.hID and O.mID=M.mID and
                M.story = '1';

subdivisionsOfferOther :=
        select  distinct O.sName
        from    offered O, model M
        where   O.hID=M.hID and O.mID=M.mID and
                M.story <> '1';

select  *
from    subdivision S
where   exists
        (select *
        from    subdivisionsOfferSingle O
        where   S.sName=O.sName) and
        not exists
                (select *
                from    subdivisionsOfferOther D
                where   S.sName=D.sName);
```

√Q2.2: List all the homebuilders who offer single-story models with at least 2000 square feet in subdivisions located in 'Tempe':

(hName, hPhone)

Relational Algebra

```
homebuildersOffering :=
    π_{hID,sName} ((σ_{story='1' and sqft>2000} (model)) ⋈ offered);
tempeSubdivisions := π_{sName} (σ_{sCity='Tempe'} (subdivision));
π_{hName,hPhone} (homebuilder ⋈
    (homebuildersOffering ⋈ tempeSubdivisions) );
```

DRC

```
{ HName, HPhone | (exists HID, MID, SName, Sqft)
    (homebuilder(HID, HName, _, _, _, HPhone) and
    model(HID, MID, _, Sqft, '1') and Sqft > 2000 and
    offered(SName, HID, MID, _) and
    subdivision(SName, 'Tempe', _) ) };
```

TRC

```
{ H.hName, H.hPhone | (exists M, O, S)
    (homebuilder(H) and model(M) and
    offered(O) and subdivision(S) and
    H.hID=M.hID and M.story='1' and M.sqft > 2000 and
    M.hID=O.hID and M.mID=O.mID and
    O.sName=S.sName and S.sCity='Tempe') };
```

SQL

```
select  H.hName, H.hPhone
from    homebuilder H, model M, offered O, subdivision S
where   H.hID=M.hID and M.story='1' and M.sqft > 2000 and
                M.hID=O.hID and M.mID=O.mID and
        O.sName=S.sName and S.sCity='Tempe';
```

√Q2.3: Which lots in the 'Terraces' subdivision are available (i.e., not sold)?

(lotNum, lStAddr, lSize, lPremium)

Relational Algebra

allTerracesLots := $\pi_{\text{sName,lotNum}}$ ($\sigma_{\text{sName='Terraces'}}$ (lot));
soldTerracesLots := $\pi_{\text{sName,lotNum}}$ ($\sigma_{\text{sName='Terraces'}}$ (sold));
availableTerracesLots := allTerracesLots − soldTerracesLots;
$\pi_{\text{lotNum,lStAddr,lSize,lPremium}}$ (availableTerracesLots $\bowtie$ lot);

DRC

```
{ LotNum, LStAddr, LSize, LPremium |
    lot('Terraces', LotNum, LStAddr, LSize, LPremium) and
    not sold('Terraces', LotNum, _, _, _) };
```

TRC

```
{ L.lotNum, L.lStAddr, L.lSize, L.lPremium |
    lot(L) and L.sName='Terraces' and
    not (exists S)(sold(S) and S.sName=L.sName and
        S.lotNum=L.lotNum) };
```

SQL

```
select  L.lotNum, L.lStAddr, L.lSize, L.lPremium
from    lot L
where   L.sName='Terraces' and
        not exists
        (select *
        from    sold S
        where   S.sName=L.sName and S.lotNum=L.lotNum);
```

√Q2.4: Which model(s) are not currently offered in any subdivision?

(hName, mName)

Relational Algebra

allModels := $\pi_{\text{hID,mID}}$ (model);
offeredModels := $\pi_{\text{hID,mID}}$ (offered);
$\pi_{\text{hName,mName}}$
(((allModels − offeredModels) $\bowtie$ model) $\bowtie$ homebuilder);

DRC

```
{HName, MName | (exists HID, MID)
    (homebuilder(HID, HName, _, _, _, _) and
    model(HID, MID, MName, _, _) and
    not offered(_, HID, MID, _) ) };
```

TRC

```
{ H.hName, M.mName |
    homebuilder(H) and model(M) and H.hID = M.hID and
    not (exists O)(offered(O) and M.hID=O.hID and
        M.mID=O.mID) };
```

SQL

```
select  H.hName, M.mName
from    homebuilder H, model M
where   H.hID = M.hID and
        not exists
        (select *
        from    offered O
        where   M.hID=O.hID and M.mID=O.mID);
```

√Q2.5: Which subdivisions offer models from more than one homebuilder?

```
(sName, sCity, sZip)
```

Relational Algebra

offersBuilder := $\pi_{\text{sName,hID}}$ (offered);
offersBuilderCopy(sNameCopy, hIDCopy) := offersBuilder;
offersMoreThanOneBuilder :=
π_{sName} (offersBuilder $\bowtie_{\text{sName=sNameCopy and hID<>hIDCopy}}$ offersBuilderCopy);
offersMoreThanOneBuilder $\bowtie$ subdivision;

DRC

```
{ SName, SCity, SZip |
    subdivision(SName, SCity, SZip) and
    (exists HID1, HID2)
        (offered(SName, HID1, _, _) and
```

```
        offered(SName, HID2, _, _) and
        HID1 <> HID2 ) };
```

TRC

```
{ S | subdivision(S) and
    (exists O1, O2)
        (offered(O1) and O1.sName=S.sName and
        offered(O2) and O2.sName=S.sName and
        O1.hID <> O2.hID) };
```

SQL

```
countBuilders(sName, numberBuilders) :=
        select    sName, count(distinct hID)
        from      offered
        group by  sName;

select  *
from    subdivision S
where   exists
        (select *
        from    countBuilders C
        where   C.sName= S.sName and C.numberBuilders > 1);
```

√Q2.6: Which models are offered in only one subdivision?

```
(hName, mName)
```

Relational Algebra

offersModel := $\pi_{\text{hID,mID,sName}}$ (offered);
offersModelCopy(hIDCopy, mIDCopy, sNameCopy) := offersModel;
offeredMoreThanOneSubdivision := $\pi_{\text{hID,mID}}$
    (offersModel $\bowtie_{\text{hID=hIDCopy and mID=mIDCopy and sName<>sNameCopy}}$
        offersModelCopy);
offeredOnlyOneSubdivision :=
    ($\pi_{\text{hID,mID}}$ (offersModel)) − offeredMoreThanOneSubdivision;
$\pi_{\text{hName,mName}}$ ((offeredOnlyOneSubdivision $\bowtie$ model)
        $\bowtie$ homebuilder);

DRC

```
{HName,MName | (exists HID, MID, SName)
    (homebuilder(HID,HName,_,_,_,_) and
```

```
    model(HID,MID,MName,_,_) and
    offered(SName,HID,MID,_) and
    not (exists AnotherSName)
        (offered(AnotherSName,HID,MID,_) and
        SName<>AnotherSName))};
```

TRC

```
{H.hName, M.mName | (exists O)
    (homebuilder(H) and model(M) and M.hID=H.hID and
    offered(O) and O.hID=M.hID and O.mID=M.mID and
    not (exists F)
        (offered(F) and F.hID=O.hID and
        F.mID=O.mID and F.sName<>O.sName))};
```

SQL

```
modelsOnlyOneSubdivision :=
        select    hID, mID, count(*)
        from      offered O
        group by  hID, mID
        having    count(*) = 1;

select  H.hName, M.mName
from    homebuilder H, model M, modelsOnlyOneSubdivision S
where   H.hID = M.hID and M.hID=S.hID and M.mID=S.mID;
```

√Q2.7: Which model(s) offered in the 'Foothills' subdivision has the maximum square footage?

(hName, mName, sqft)

Relational Algebra

foothillsModels := $\pi_{\text{hID,hName,mID,mName,sqft}}$
    $(((\sigma_{\text{sName='Foothills'}}\ (\text{offered})) \bowtie \text{model}) \bowtie \text{homebuilder})$;
foothillsSqft := π_{sqft} (foothillsModels);
foothillsSqftCopy(sqftCopy) := foothillsSqft;
notMaxFoothillsSqft :=
    $\pi_{\text{sqft}}\ (\text{foothillsSqft} \bowtie_{\text{sqft<sqftCopy}} \text{foothillsSqftCopy})$;
maxFoothillsSqft := foothillsSqft − notMaxFoothillsSqft;
$\pi_{\text{hName,mName,sqft}}\ (\text{maxFoothillsSqft} \bowtie \text{foothillsModels})$;

DRC

```
foothillsModels :=
    { HID, MID, Sqft |
        offered('Foothills', HID, MID, _) and
        model(HID, MID, _, Sqft, _) };

maxSqftFoothillsModels :=
    {HID, MID, Sqft |
        foothillsModels(HID, MID, Sqft) and
        not (exists S)
            (foothillsModels(_, _, S) and S > Sqft)};

{ HName, MName, Sqft | (exists HID, MID)
    (maxSqftFoothillsModels(HID, MID, Sqft) and
    homebuilder(HID, HName, _, _, _, _) and
    model(HID, MID, MName, Sqft, _)) };
```

TRC

```
foothillsModels :=
    { M.hID, M.mID, M.sqft |
        model(M) and (exists O)
        (offered(O) and O.sName='Foothills' and
        O.hID=M.hID and O.mID=M.mID) };

maxSqftFoothillsModels :=
    {F | foothillsModels(F) and
        not (exists M)
            (foothillsModels(M) and M.sqft > F.sqft) };

{ H.hName, M.mName, S.sqft |
    homebuilder(H) and model(M) and
    maxSqftFoothillsModels(S) and
    H.hID=S.hID and M.hID=S.hID and M.mID=S.mID };
```

SQL

```
foothillsModels :=
        select  M.hID, M.mID, M.sqft
        from    model M, offered O
        where   M.hID=O.hID and M.mID=O.mID and
                O.sName = 'Foothills';
```

```
maxSqftFoothills(maxsqft) :=
        select  max(sqft)
        from    foothillsModels;

maxSqftFoothillsModels :=
        select  F.hID, F.mID, F.sqft
        from    foothillsModels F, maxSqftFoothills M
        where   F.sqft=M.maxsqft;

select  H.hName, M.mName, S.sqft
from    homebuilder H, model M, maxSqftFoothillsModels S
where   H.hID=S.hID and M.hID=S.hID and M.mID=S.mID;
```

√Q2.8: Which subdivision offers all the models by the homebuilder 'Homer'?

```
(sName, sCity, sZip)
```

Relational Algebra

homerHID := $\pi_{\texttt{hID}}$ ($\sigma_{\text{hName='Homer'}}$ (homebuilder));
homerModels := $\pi_{\texttt{hID,mID}}$ (homerHID $\bowtie$ model);
offersHomerModels := $\pi_{\text{sName},\texttt{hID,mID}}$ (homerModels $\bowtie$ offered);
offersAllHomerModels := offersHomerModels $\div$ homerModels;
subdivision $\bowtie$ offersAllHomerModels;

DRC

```
{SName,SCity,SZip | (exists HomerHID)
    (subdivision(SName,SCity,SZip) and
    homebuilder(HomerHID,'Homer',_,_,_,_) and
    offered(SName,HomerHID,_,_) and
    not (exists MID)
        (model(HomerHID,MID,_,_,_) and
        not offered(SName,HomerHID,MID,_)))};
```

TRC

```
homerModels :=
    { M.hID, M.mID | (exists H)
        (homebuilder(H) and H.hName='Homer' and
        model(M) and M.hID=H.hID) };
```

```
{ S | subdivision(S) and (exists O,M)
    (offered(O) and homerModels(M) and
    S.sName=O.sName and O.hID=M.hID) and
    not (exists H) (homerModels(H) and
        not (exists F) (offered(F) and
            F.sName=S.sName and F.hID=H.hID and
            F.mID=H.mID)) };
```

SQL

```
homerModels :=
        select  M.hID, M.mID
        from    homebuilder H, model M
        where   H.hName='Homer' and H.hID=M.hID;

offersHomerModels :=
        select  S.sName
        from    subdivision S
        where   exists
                (select *
                from    offered O, homerModels M
                where   S.sName=O.sName and O.hID=M.hID) ;

select  S.sName, S.sCity, S.sZip
from    subdivision S, offersHomerModels O
where   S.sName=O.sName and
        not exists
                (select *
                from    homerModels H
                where   not exists
                        (select *
                        from    offered F
                        where   F.sName=S.sName and
                                F.hID=H.hID and
                                F.mID=H.mID));
```

√Q2.9: For each subdivision, find the number of models offered and the average, minimum, and maximum price of the models offered at that subdivision. Display the result in descending order on the average price of a home.

```
(sName, sCity, numberOfModels, avgPrice, minPrice, maxPrice)
```

SQL

```
select    S.sName, S.sCity, count(*),
          avg(O.price), min(O.price), max(O.price)
from      offered O, subdivision S
where     O.sName=S.sName
group by  S.sName, S.sCity
order by  4 desc;
```

√Q2.10: For each subdivision, find the total of lot premiums for lots that are available. Display the result in ascending order on the total of lot premiums:

```
(sName, sCity, totalLotPremium)
```

SQL

```
select    S.sName, S.sCity, sum(L.lPremium)
from      subdivision S, lot L
where     S.sName=L.sName and
          not exists
                (select *
                 from    sold D
                 where   D.sName=L.sName and
                         D.lotNum=L.lotNum)
group by  S.sName, S.sCity
order by  3;
```

6.3 INVESTMENT PORTFOLIO

This simplified Investment Portfolio case study maintains information regarding clients that invest in stocks and mutual funds. Each client has a unique taxpayer identification number. A client may invest in stocks or mutual funds.

A stock is uniquely identified by its ticker, which is its symbol on the stock exchange. The name of issue for a stock is the name of the company. A stock has a rating, which is an assessment of the stock. The principal business of a stock denotes the primary business from which the company obtains its revenue. There are several prices associated with a stock. Besides the current price of a stock, the high and low price ranges are recorded for the calendar year. The return value for a stock, which is the price appreciation, is recorded for the prior year and five-year period.

A mutual fund is also uniquely identified by a ticker symbol and has a fund name. The principal objective of the fund is also recorded (e.g., 'G' for growth, 'I' for income, and 'S' for stability). Similar to stocks, mutual funds record a current offering price and a high and low price range. A percent yield from investment income is also maintained. A mutual fund may be associated with at most one fund family.

A fund family has a unique identification number and the company's name and address. A fund family, as its name implies, can have many associated mutual funds, but must have at least one mutual fund.

CONCEPTUAL DESIGN

Based on the high-level introduction to the INVESTMENT PORTFOLIO enterprise, assume the following:

- The characteristics of a client include a unique taxpayer identification number, a name, and an address. A client can invest in many stocks and in many mutual funds.
- The characteristics of a stock include the stock's unique ticker on the stock exchange and additional descriptive properties that include the name of issue, a rating, the principal business, a high and low price range, the current price, and return values for the prior year and 5-year period.
- The characteristics of a mutual fund include the mutual fund's unique ticker and additional descriptive properties that include the name of the fund, its principal objective, the high and low price range, the current offering price, and the fund's yield. A mutual fund may be associated with at most one fund family.
- The characteristics of a fund family include a unique identification, a name, and an address. A fund family may have many mutual funds and must be associated with at least one mutual fund.

Figure 6.5 provides an ER diagram corresponding to the conceptual design of the INVESTMENT PORTFOLIO enterprise. The entities are summarized in Table 6.7, and the relationships are summarized in Table 6.8. The entities `client`, `stock`, `mutualFund`, and `fundFamily` are strong entities having unique identifiers across the entire database. The relationships `stockPortfolio` and `mutualFundPortfolio` have an M:N cardinality ratio, since a client can invest in many stocks or mutual funds, and a stock or mutual fund can be part of many portfolios. There is a descriptive attribute on these M:N relationships, which indicates the number of shares of the investment that the client's portfolio contains. The `hasFundFamily` relationship has a 1:N cardinality ratio, since a fund family can have many mutual funds, but a mutual fund may be associated with at most one fund family. The total participation of the `fundFamily` entity in the `hasFundFamily` relationship indicates that a fund family must have at least one mutual fund.

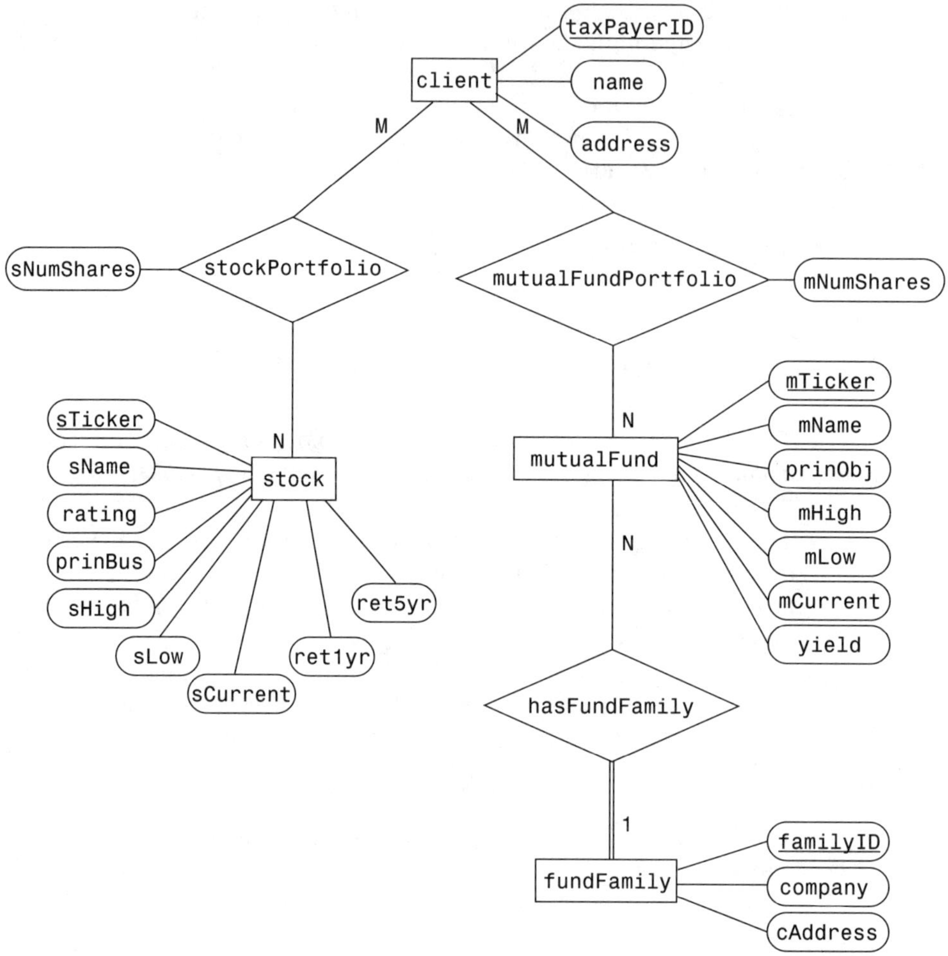

Figure 6.5 INVESTMENT PORTFOLIO ER diagram.

RELATIONAL SCHEMA

Figure 6.6 provides the relational schema for the INVESTMENT PORTFOLIO enterprise given by the conceptual design in Figure 6.5. The schema includes a table for each entity (`client`, `stock`, `mutualFund`, and `fundFamily`). The M:N portfolio relationships between a client and the stocks and mutual funds that they own are mapped as the tables `stockPortfolio` and `mutualFundPortfolio`, respectively. The 1:N relationship `hasFundFamily`, relating a fund family to its associated mutual fund, is mapped as the `familyID` attribute of the `mutualFund` table, since a mutual fund belongs to exactly one fund family.

TABLE 6.7 INVESTMENT PORTFOLIO entity summary.

Entity	Attribute	Type	Description
client	taxPayerID	C	The unique taxpayer ID that identifies a client.
	name	C	The name of the client.
	address	C	The address of the client.
stock	sTicker	C	The unique ID to identify a stock.
	sName	C	The name of the company to which the stock belongs.
	rating	C	The rating of the stock with values limited to 'NR' (no rating), 'C' (nonpaying issue), or 'A' (backed).
	prinBus	C	The principal business in which the company engages.
	sHigh	N	The highest rate of the stock.
	sLow	N	The lowest rate of the stock.
	sCurrent	N	The current rate of the stock.
	ret1Yr	N	The returns made by the stock over one year.
	ret5Yr	N	The returns made by the stock over five years.
mutualFund	mTicker	C	The unique ID to identify a mutual fund.
	mName	C	The name of the mutual fund.
	prinObj	C	The principal objective of the fund with values limited to 'G' (growth), 'I' (income), and 'S' (stability).
	mHigh	N	The highest rate of the mutual fund.
	mLow	N	The lowest rate of the mutual fund.
	mCurrent	N	The current rate of the mutual fund.
	yield	N	The yield made by the mutual fund.
fundFamily	familyID	C	The unique ID to identify the fund family.
	company	C	The name of the fund family.
	cAddress	C	The address of the fund family.

```
client(taxPayerID, name, address)
stock(sTicker, sName, rating, prinBus, sHigh, sLow, sCurrent, ret1Yr, ret5Yr)
mutualFund(mTicker,  mName, prinObj, mHigh, mLow, mCurrent, yield, familyID)
fundFamily(familyID, company, cAddress)
stockPortfolio(taxPayerID, sTicker, sNumShares)
mutualFundPortfolio(taxPayerID, mTicker, mNumShares)
```

Figure 6.6 INVESTMENT PORTFOLIO relational schema.

QUERIES

Table 6.9 provides a list of relevant queries over the INVESTMENT PORTFOLIO database used to provide a side-by-side comparison of the query languages. Queries 1 through 8 are answered in all four query languages, but the complex aggregation queries 9 and 10 can only be answered in SQL.

TABLE 6.8 INVESTMENT PORTFOLIO relationship summary.

Relationship	Description
stockPortfolio	An M: N relationship between a stock and a client. A client can have many shares of a stock, and a stock has many shareholders. The `sNumShares` attribute, which is a numeric type, represents the number of shares of a stock that a client has.
mutualFundPortfolio	An M: N relationship between a mutual fund and a client. A client can have many shares of a mutual fund, and a mutual fund has many shareholders. The `mNumShares` attribute, which is a numeric type, represents the number of shares of a mutual fund that a client has.
hasFundFamily	A 1: N relationship between a mutual fund and fund family. A fund family may have many mutual funds and must be associated with at least one mutual fund. A mutual fund is associated with exactly one fund family.

TABLE 6.9 INVESTMENT PORTFOLIO query summary.

Query	**Query Description**
Q3.1	What clients have invested in which 'A' rated stocks?
Q3.2	Which clients invest in both stocks whose principal business is 'Technology' and mutual funds having growth ('G') as a principal objective?
Q3.3	What clients have not invested in mutual funds with income ('I') as a principal objective?
Q3.4	Which clients invest in stocks but not in mutual funds?
Q3.5	Which clients have more than one no-rating ('NR') stock?
Q3.6	Which clients invest in only one mutual fund with stability ('S') as a principal objective?
Q3.7	Which mutual funds have the minimum current rate?
Q3.8	What clients have invested in all of the mutual funds within the 'Fictitious' fund family?
Q3.9	For each client that invests in stocks, display the average, minimum, and maximum one-year returns on the stocks they own. Display the result in ascending order on average one-year returns.
Q3.10	For each client that invests in mutual funds, display the sum of the number of shares of mutual funds that they own within each principal objective category. Display the result in descending order on the number of shares.

√Q3.1: What clients have invested in which 'A' rated stocks?

```
(taxPayerID, name, sTicker, sName)
```

Relational Algebra

$\pi_{\texttt{taxPayerID,name,sTicker,sName}}$
((($\sigma_{\texttt{rating='A'}}$ (stock)) ⋈ stockPortfolio) ⋈ client);

DRC

```
{ TaxPayerID, Name, STicker, SName |
   client(TaxPayerID, Name, _) and
   stockPortfolio(TaxPayerID, STicker, _) and
   stock(STicker, SName, 'A', _, _, _, _, _, _) };
```

TRC

```
{ C.taxPayerID, C.name, S.sTicker, S.sName |
   client(C) and stock(S) and
   (exists P)
      (stockPortfolio(P) and
      S.rating = 'A' and
      S.sTicker = P.sTicker and
      P.taxPayerID = C.taxPayerID) };
```

SQL

```
select  C.taxPayerID, C.name, S.sTicker, S.sName
from    client C, stock S, stockPortfolio P
where   S.rating = 'A' and
        S.sTicker = P.sTicker and
        P.taxPayerID = C.taxPayerID;
```

√Q3.2: Which clients invest in both stocks whose principal business is 'Technology' and mutual funds having growth ('G') as a principal objective?

(taxPayerID, name)

Relational Algebra

technologyClients := $\pi_{\texttt{taxPayerID}}$
(($\sigma_{\texttt{prinBus='Technology'}}$ (stock)) ⋈ stockPortfolio);
growthClients := $\pi_{\texttt{taxPayerID}}$
(($\sigma_{\texttt{prinObj='G'}}$ (mutualFund)) ⋈ mutualFundPortfolio);
$\pi_{\texttt{taxPayerID,name}}$
((technologyClients ∩ growthClients) ⋈ client);

DRC

```
{ TaxPayerID, Name | (exists STicker, MTicker)
    (client(TaxPayerID, Name, _) and
    stockPortfolio(TaxPayerID, STicker, _) and
    stock(STicker, _, _, 'Technology', _, _, _, _, _) and
    mutualFundPortfolio(TaxPayerID, MTicker, _) and
    mutualFund(MTicker, _, 'G', _, _, _, _, _)) };
```

TRC

```
technologyClients :=
    { P.taxPayerID | stockPortfolio(P) and (exists S)
        (stock(S) and S.prinBus = 'Technology' and
        S.sTicker = P.sTicker) };
growthClients :=
    { P.taxPayerID | mutualFundPortfolio(P) and (exists M)
        (mutualFund(M) and M.prinObj = 'G' and
        M.mTicker = P.mTicker) };
{ C.taxPayerID, C.name | client(C) and (exists T,G)
    (technologyClients(T) and T.taxPayerID=C.taxPayerID and
    growthClients(G) and G.taxPayerID=C.taxPayerID)};
```

SQL

```
technologyClients :=
        select  distinct P.taxPayerID
        from    stock S, stockPortfolio P
        where   S.prinBus = 'Technology' and
                S.sTicker = P.sTicker;
growthClients :=
        select  distinct P.taxPayerID
        from    mutualFund M, mutualFundPortfolio P
        where   M.prinObj = 'G' and M.mTicker = P.mTicker;
technologyGrowthClients :=
        (select * from technologyClients)
        intersect
        (select * from growthClients);

select  C.taxPayerID, C.name
from    client C
where   C.taxPayerID in
            (select * from technologyGrowthClients);
```

√Q3.3: What clients have not invested in mutual funds with income ('I') as a principal objective?

```
(taxPayerID, name)
```

Relational Algebra

investI := $\pi_{\text{taxPayerID}}$
    (($\sigma_{\text{prinObj='I'}}$(mutualFund)) $\bowtie$ mutualFundPortfolio);
notInvestI := ($\pi_{\text{taxPayerID}}$ (client)) − investI;
$\pi_{\text{taxPayerID,name}}$ (client $\bowtie$ notInvestI);

DRC

```
{ TaxPayerID, Name |
    client(TaxPayerID, Name, _) and not (exists MTicker)
        (mutualFundPortfolio(TaxPayerID, MTicker, _) and
        mutualFund(MTicker, _, 'I', _, _, _, _, _)) };
```

TRC

```
{ C.taxPayerID, C.name |
    client(C) and not (exists M,P)
        (mutualFund(M) and mutualFundPortfolio(P) and
        M.prinObj='I' and
        M.mTicker=P.mTicker and
        P.taxPayerID=C.taxPayerID) };
```

SQL

```
select  C.taxPayerID, C.name
from    client C
where   C.taxPayerID not in
        (select P.taxPayerID
        from    mutualFund M, mutualFundPortfolio P
        where   M.prinObj='I' and M.mTicker=P.mTicker);
```

√Q3.4: Which clients invest in stocks, but not in mutual funds?

```
(taxPayerID, name)
```

Relational Algebra

$$\begin{array}{l}\texttt{stocksNotMutualFunds :=}\\ \quad (\pi_{\texttt{taxPayerID}}\ \texttt{(stockPortfolio))} -\\ \quad (\pi_{\texttt{taxPayerID}}\ \texttt{(mutualFundPortfolio));}\\ \pi_{\texttt{taxPayerID,name}}\ \texttt{(client} \bowtie \texttt{stocksNotMutualFunds);}\end{array}$$

DRC

```
{ TaxPayerID, Name |
    client(TaxPayerID, Name, _) and
    (exists STicker)
        (stockPortfolio(TaxPayerID, STicker, _) and
        stock(STicker, _, _, _, _, _, _, _, _))
    and not (exists MTicker)
        (mutualFundPortfolio(TaxPayerID, MTicker, _) and
        mutualFund(MTicker, _, _, _, _, _, _, _)) };
```

TRC

```
{ C.taxPayerID, C.name | client(C) and
    (exists SP)(stockPortfolio(SP) and
        SP.taxPayerID=C.taxPayerID) and
        not (exists MP)(mutualFundPortfolio(MP) and
            MP.taxPayerID=C.taxPayerID) };
```

SQL

```
select  C.taxPayerID, C.name
from    client C
where   C.taxPayerID in
                (select SP.taxPayerID
                from    stockPortfolio SP) and
        C.taxPayerID not in
                (select MP.taxPayerID
                from    mutualFundPortfolio MP);
```

√Q3.5: Which clients have more than one no-rating ('NR') stock?

```
(taxPayerID, name)
```

Relational Algebra

investNR := $\pi_{\text{taxPayerID,sTicker}}$
    (($\sigma_{\text{rating='NR'}}$ (stock)) $\bowtie$ stockPortfolio);
investNRCopy(taxPayerIDCopy, sTickerCopy) := investNR;
moreThanOneNR := $\pi_{\text{taxPayerID}}$
    (investNR $\bowtie_{\text{taxPayerID=taxPayerIDCopy and sTicker<>sTickerCopy}}$
        investNRCopy);
$\pi_{\text{taxPayerID,name}}$ (client $\bowtie$ moreThanOneNR);

DRC

```
investNR :=
    { TaxPayerID, STicker |
        client(TaxPayerID, _, _) and
        stockPortfolio(TaxPayerID, STicker, _) and
        stock(STicker, _, 'NR', _, _, _, _, _, _) };

{ TaxPayerID, Name |
    client(TaxPayerID, Name, _) and
    (exists STicker1, STicker2)
        (investNR(TaxPayerID, STicker1) and
        investNR(TaxPayerID, STicker2) and
        STicker1 <> STicker2) };
```

TRC

```
investNR :=
    { C.taxPayerID, S.sTicker |
        client(C) and stock(S) and S.rating='NR' and
        (exists P)
            (stockPortfolio(P) and
            P.taxPayerID=C.taxPayerID and
            P.sTicker=S.sTicker) };

{ C.taxPayerID, C.name |
    client(C) and
    (exists I1, I2)
        (investNR(I1) and I1.taxPayerID=C.taxPayerID and
        investNR(I2) and I2.taxPayerID=C.taxPayerID and
        I1.sTicker <> I2.sTicker) };
```

SQL

```
moreThanOneNRstock(taxPayerID, numNRstocks) :=
        select    P.taxPayerID, count(*)
        from      stock S, stockPortfolio P
        where     S.rating='NR' and P.sTicker=S.sTicker
        group by  P.taxPayerID
        having    count(*)>1;

select  C.taxPayerID, C.name
from    client C
where   C.taxPayerID in
        (select M.taxPayerID
        from    moreThanOneNRstock M);
```

√Q3.6: Which clients invest in only one mutual fund with stability ('S') as a principal objective?

```
(taxPayerID, name)
```

Relational Algebra

$\text{investS} := \pi_{\text{taxPayerID,mTicker}}$
$\quad ((\sigma_{\text{prinObj='S'}}(\text{mutualFund})) \bowtie \text{mutualFundPortfolio});$
$\text{investSCopy(taxPayerIDCopy, mTickerCopy)} := \text{investS};$
$\text{moreThanOneS} := \pi_{\text{taxPayerID}}$
$\quad (\text{investS} \bowtie_{\text{taxPayerID=taxPayerIDCopy and mTicker<>mTickerCopy}}$
$\qquad \text{investSCopy});$
$\text{onlyOneS} := (\pi_{\text{taxPayerID}}(\text{investS})) - \text{moreThanOneS};$
$\pi_{\text{taxPayerID,name}}(\text{client} \bowtie \text{onlyOneS});$

DRC

```
investS(taxPayerID, mTicker) :=
    { TaxPayerID, MTicker |
        mutualFund(MTicker, _, 'S', _, _, _, _, _) and
        mutualFundPortfolio(TaxPayerID, MTicker, _) };

{ TaxPayerID, Name | (exists MTicker)
    (client(TaxPayerID, Name, _) and
    investS(TaxPayerID, MTicker) and
    not (exists M)
        (investS(TaxPayerID, M) and M<>MTicker)) };
```

TRC

```
investS(taxPayerID, mTicker) :=
    { P.taxPayerID, P.mTicker |
        mutualFundPortfolio(P) and (exists M)
            (mutualFund(M) and
            M.mTicker=P.mTicker and
            M.prinObj='S') };

{ C.taxPayerID, C.name | client(C) and
    (exists I1)(investS(I1) and I1.taxPayerID=C.taxPayerID and
        not (exists I2) (investS(I2) and
            I2.taxPayerID=C.taxPayerID and
            I1.mTicker<>I2.mTicker)) };
```

SQL

```
countSmutualFunds(taxPayerID, numSmutualFunds) :=
        select   P.taxPayerID, count(*)
        from     mutualFund M, mutualFundPortfolio P
        where    M.prinObj='S' and P.mTicker=M.mTicker
        group by P.taxPayerID;

select  C.taxPayerID, C.name
from    client C, countSmutualFunds S
where   C.taxPayerID=S.taxPayerID and S.numSmutualFunds=1;
```

√Q3.7: Which mutual funds have the minimum current rate?

```
(mTicker, mName, mCurrent)
```

Relational Algebra

currentRate := π_{mCurrent} (mutualFund);
currentRateCopy(mCurrentCopy) := currentRate;
notMinimumRate := π_{mCurrent}
    (currentRate $\bowtie_{\text{mCurrent>mCurrentCopy}}$ currentRateCopy);
minimumRate := currentRate − notMinimumRate;
$\pi_{\text{mTicker,mName,mCurrent}}$ (mutualFund $\bowtie$ minimumRate);

DRC

```
{ MTicker, MName, MCurrent |
```

```
    mutualFund(MTicker, MName, _, _, _, MCurrent, _, _) and
    not (exists C) (mutualFund(_, _, _, _, _, C, _, _) and
        C < MCurrent) };
```

TRC

```
{ M.mTicker, M.mName, M.mCurrent |
    mutualFund(M) and
    not (exists F)(mutualFund(F) and
        F.mCurrent < M.mCurrent) };
```

SQL

```
minMFcurrent(minCurrent) :=
        select  min(M.mCurrent)
        from    mutualFund M;

select  M.mTicker, M.mName, M.mCurrent
from    mutualFund M
where   M.mCurrent = (select minCurrent from minMFcurrent);
```

√Q3.8: What clients have invested in all of the mutual funds within the 'Fictitious' fund family?

```
(taxPayerID, name)
```

Relational Algebra

fictitiousFunds := π_{mTicker}
    (($\sigma_{\text{company='Fictitious'}}$ (fundFamily)) ⋈ mutualFund);
clientsTickersAtLeastOneFund :=
    $\pi_{\text{taxPayerID,mTicker}}$ (fictitiousFunds ⋈ mutualFundPortfolio);
clientsAtLeastOneFund :=
    $\pi_{\text{taxPayerID}}$ (clientsTickersAtLeastOneFund);
allClientsWithAllFunds :=
    clientsAtLeastOneFund × fictitiousFunds;
clientsNotAllFunds := $\pi_{\text{taxPayerID}}$
    (allClientsWithAllFunds − clientsTickersAtLeastOneFund);
clientsAllFunds :=
    clientsAtLeastOneFund − clientsNotAllFunds;
$\pi_{\text{taxPayerID,name}}$ (client ⋈ clientsAllFunds);

DRC

```
fictitiousFunds :=
    { MTicker | (exists FID)
        (mutualFund(MTicker, _, _, _, _, _, _, FID) and
        fundFamily(FID, 'Fictitious', _)) };

{ TaxPayerID, Name |
    client(TaxPayerID, Name, _) and
    (exists FTicker)(fictitiousFunds(FTicker) and
        mutualFundPortfolio(TaxPayerID, FTicker, _)) and
    not (exists MTicker)
        (fictitiousFunds(MTicker) and
        not mutualFundPortfolio(TaxPayerID, MTicker, _)) };
```

TRC

```
fictitiousFunds :=
    { M.mTicker | (exists F)
        (mutualFund(M) and fundFamily(F) and
        F.company='Fictitious' and
        F.familyID=M.familyID) };

{ C.taxPayerID, C.name |
    client(C) and
    (exists FF, MFP)(fictitiousFunds(FF) and
        mutualFundPortfolio(MFP) and
        MFP.taxPayerID=C.taxPayerID and
        MFP.mTicker=FF.mTicker) and
    not (exists F) (fictitiousFunds(F) and
        not (exists P)
            (mutualFundPortfolio(P) and
            P.taxPayerID=C.taxPayerID and
            P.mTicker=F.mTicker)) };
```

SQL

```
fictitiousFunds :=
        select  M.mTicker
        from    mutualFund M, fundFamily F
        where   F.company='Fictitious' and
                F.familyID=M.familyID;

select  C.taxPayerID, C.name
from    client C
```

```
where   exists
                (select *
                from    fictitiousFunds FF,
                        mutualFundPortfolio MFP
                where   MFP.taxPayerID=C.taxPayerID and
                        MFP.mTicker=FF.mTicker) and
        not exists
                (select *
                from    fictitiousFunds F
                where   not exists
                        (select *
                        from    mutualFundPortfolio P
                        where   P.taxPayerID=C.taxPayerID and
                                P.mTicker=F.mTicker));
```

√Q3.9: For each client that invests in stocks, display the average, minimum, and maximum one-year returns on the stocks they own. Display the result in ascending order on average one-year returns:

```
(taxPayerID, name, avgReturn1Yr, minReturn1Yr, maxReturn1Yr)
```

SQL

```
select    C.taxPayerID, C.name, avg(S.ret1Yr),
          min(S.ret1Yr), max(S.ret1Yr)
from      client C, stockPortfolio P, stock S
where     C.taxPayerID=P.taxPayerID and P.sTicker=S.sTicker
group by  C.taxPayerID, C.name
order by  3 asc;
```

√Q3.10: For each client that invests in mutual funds, display the sum of the number of shares of mutual funds that the client owns within each principal objective category. Display the result in descending order on the number of shares:

```
(taxPayerID, name, prinObj, numShares)
```

SQL

```
sumSharesByPrincObj(taxPayerID, prinObj, numShares) :=
```

```
            select    P.taxPayerID, M.prinObj, sum(P.mNumShares)
            from      mutualFundPortfolio P, mutualFund M
            where     P.mTicker=M.mTicker
            group by  P.taxPayerID, M.prinObj;

select    C.taxPayerID, C.name, S.prinObj, S.numShares
from      sumSharesByPrincObj S, client C
where     S.taxPayerID=C.taxPayerID
order by  4 desc;
```

6.4 SUMMARY

The case studies for three enterprises presented examples illustrating various data modeling issues, such as recursive relationships in the WEB PAGE enterprise and weak entities in the NEW HOME enterprise. Each case study included a suite of 10 relevant queries over the enterprise that were expressed in all four query languages in a side-by-side comparison illustrating the characteristics of each language over various types of queries.

EXERCISES

√ Use the educational tool to check the answers to these queries.

√**6.1** Answer the following queries in each of the relational query languages over the WEB PAGE database (note that items marked by * can only be answered in SQL):

(a) Which pages contain (ftp) links to database ('M') files?

```
(webID, webTitle, url, base)
```

(b) Which pages display the graphic having the name 'lock'?

```
(webID, webTitle, url, base)
```

(c) Which pages do not contain any (ftp) links to courseware?

```
(webID, webTitle, url, base)
```

(d) Which pages contain (http) links to pages outside its base?

```
(webID, webTitle, url, base)
```

(e) Which pages display more than one 'gif' graphic?

```
(webID, webTitle, url, base)
```

(f) Which pages display only one 'jpg' graphic?

`(webID, webTitle, url, base)`

(g) Which pages have the fewest hits?

`(webID, webTitle, url, base, minHits)`

(h) Which pages display graphics of all graphic types currently contained in the database?

`(webID, webTitle, url, base)`

***(i)** How many Web pages belong to each base?
Display the results in descending order on the number of pages in the base.

`(baseWebID, baseWebTitle, url, numberOfPages)`

***(j)** For each group of Web pages belonging to the same base, find the number of (ftp) links to courseware in each category:

`(baseWebID, baseWebTitle, url, coursewareCategory, numberOfLinks)`

√**6.2** Answer the following queries in each of the relational query languages over the NEW HOME database (note that items marked by * can only be answered in SQL):

a) Which subdivisions offer models with more than 3,000 square feet?

`(sName, sCity, sZip)`

b) Which lots in the Foothills subdivision are pending ('P')?

`(lotNum, lStAddr, lSize, lPremium)`

c) Which subdivisions do not offer any models?

`(sName, sCity, sZip)`

d) Which subdivisions do not have any completed ('C') lots?

`(sName, sCity, sZip)`

(e) Which models are offered in more than one subdivision?

`(hName, mName)`

(f) Which homebuilders have only one two-story model?

`(hName)`

(g) Which model(s) in the 'Terraces' subdivision has the lowest price?

`(hName, mName, minPrice)`

(h) Is there a subdivision that offers at least one model from all the homebuilders whose headquarters are located in 'Phoenix'?

`(sName, sCity, sZip)`

*__(i)__ For each homebuilder, find the average price of all models offered. Display the result in ascending order on the average price:

`(hName, avgPrice)`

*__(j)__ For each homebuilder, find the number of subdivisions that offer models of that homebuilder. Display the result in descending order on the number of subdivisions:

`(hName, numberOfSubdivisions)`

√**6.3** Answer the following queries in each of the relational query languages over the INVESTMENT PORTFOLIO database (note that items marked by * can only be answered in SQL):

(a) What clients own more than 200 shares of which stocks?

(taxPayerID, name, sTicker, sName, sNumShares)

(b) Which stock's one-year return has outperformed its five-year return?

(sTicker, sName, prinBus, ret1Yr, ret5Yr)

(c) What clients have not invested in stocks with 'Technology' as its principal business?

(taxPayerID, name)

(d) Which clients invest in mutual funds, but not in individual stocks?

(taxPayerID, name)

(e) Which clients invest in more than one mutual fund with growth ('G') as its principal objective?

(taxPayerID, name)

(f) Which clients have only one 'A'-rating stock?

(taxPayerID, name)

(g) Which stocks have the maximum one-year return?

(sTicker, sName, prinBus, ret1Yr)

(h) Which clients have invested in *all* stocks having a one-year return greater than its five-year return?

(taxPayerID, name)

***(i)** For each mutual fund, find the number of clients that invest in the fund and the total number of shares of the fund invested by all clients. Display the result in descending order on the number of clients:

(mTicker, mName, numberOfClients, totalShares)

***(j)** For each client that invests in stocks, find the sum of the number of shares of stocks they own with each stock rating. Display the result in ascending order on stock rating within an alphabetical listing by client:

(taxPayerID, name, stockRating, numberOfRatingShares)

Chapter 7

Microsoft Access

Microsoft Access is a popular PC-based relational database product. For personal and small business use, Access provides a powerful database that is easy to use, since it has graphical user interface (GUI) for data definition, population, and querying. Since the definition of the database constraints plays a role in the querying capabilities of Access, an overview of data definition precedes the more detailed discussion on the query languages of Access. A brief discussion of data population is also included, since the database must be populated after it is defined and before it is queried. The six example queries over the EMPLOYEE TRAINING enterprise continue to illustrate the query language features.

7.1 DATA DEFINITION

The GUI for data definition consists of two main components: one to define the table and its attributes, which are called *fields* in Access, and another to define the referential integrity or *relationships* between tables. Note that Access also provides the capability to specify data definition using SQL syntax, which can be found under the `SQL Specific` item on the `Query` menu.

Figure 7.1 shows the table design view of the `employee` table. For each field of the table, its name and data type are specified along with additional field properties. Access has the following data types: text, memo and hyperlink; number, currency, and autonumber; date–time and yes–no. The following is an abbreviated overview of the additional properties of a field (in the context of a text data type), and you are encouraged to read the Access online documentation for more information:

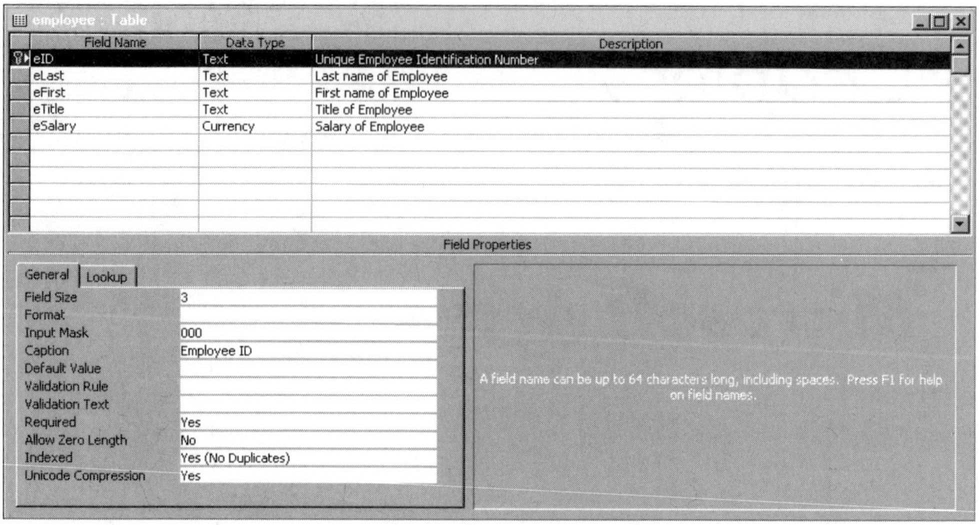

Figure 7.1 Table `employee` design view.

- Size

  Associated with a data type is a size property, which specifies additional characteristics for that data type, such as the length of a text field or the choice of representation for a number (byte, integer, long integer, etc.)

- Format

  The format property specifies how data is displayed. Access provides predefined display formats for some of the data types, such as dates, currency, and yes–no fields. Customizable formats are also possible.

- Input mask

  The input mask property defines input constraints on the data, such as constraints on a text field. For example, in the United States, each individual has a taxpayer identification number that consists of nine digits. The input mask for such a field would be 000000000, since a 0 indicates that the position in the string must be a digit (0–9). As another example of a constraint, the letter L denotes that the position in the string must be a letter.

- Caption

  The caption is a default label for the field, which is generally more descriptive than the attribute name.

- Validation Rule

  The validation rule allows for the specification of additional data constraints beyond the input mask. For example, a validation rule for a salary attribute can check that the salary value is in an appropriate range.

- Validation Text

  The validation text is the text that is displayed when the validation rule is violated, such as 'Salary out of range' for the preceding validation rule.
- Required

  The required property defines whether a value is required in the field.
- Allow Zero Length

  The allow-zero-length property indicates whether a zero-length string is allowed for a text, memo or hyperlink field.
- Indexed

  The indexed property indicates whether an index is defined on the field. An index is a mechanism that provides a more efficient context search based on the field. Access allows three types of index options: no index, index with duplicates allowed, and index with no duplicates. A primary key field for a table will have an index with no duplicates allowed. Whether other fields have an index is a design decision to be made by the database admininstrator, based on the knowledge of the database application. For example, if a search on the last name of an employee is a common query, then an index with duplicates allowed should be defined on the field.
- Unicode Compression

  The unicode-compression property is defined for a text–memo–hyperlink field, which defaults to automatically compress the textual data to save space.

Table 7.1 summarizes the definition of the EMPLOYEE TRAINING database schema in Access. All of the primary keys have a unique index and an input mask specified for constraining data input. Primary key fields are defined graphically in Access by selecting the field or fields that form the primary key and clicking on the key icon on the toolbar. A unique index, which is indicated by an indexed field property of "Yes (No Duplicates)," is automatically created when a primary key is defined. Since the titles of the technology areas and training courses should be unique, a unique index is also defined for the `aTitle` and `cTitle` fields. In the `takes` table, an index is defined for each field, since common queries are expected to find which employees took what courses on certain dates. The fields that are foreign keys must be defined with data types, formats, and input masks that are consistent with the definition of the primary key that it references. For example, the `aLeadID` field of the `technologyArea` table is defined to be a three-digit text field identical to the `employee.eID` definition. Although not used in the `Employee Training` implementation, Access provides an `AutoNumber` data type, which is used for incremental generation of a unique numeric, primary key value. A foreign key that references an `AutoNumber` primary key must be defined as a `Numeric` data type with a field size of `Long Integer`.

The field properties define a constraint for that field of the table. To define constraints relating fields of the same table, Access provides for the definition of a

TABLE 7.1 Summary of EMPLOYEE TRAINING schema definition in Access.

Table	Field Name	Data Type	Size	Input Mask	Indexed
employee	eID	Text	3	000	Yes (Unique)
	eLast	Text	30		No
	eFirst	Text	20		No
	eTitle	Text	30		Yes (Duplicates)
	eSalary	Number	Currency		No
technologyArea	aID	Text	2	LL	Yes (Unique)
	aTitle	Text	25		Yes (Unique)
	aURL	Hyperlink	50		No
	aLeadID	Text	3	000	Yes (Unique)
trainingCourse	cID	Text	4	LL00	Yes (Unique)
	cTitle	Text	25		Yes (Unique)
	cHours	Number	Integer		No
	areaID	Text	2	LL	Yes (Duplicates)
takes	eID	Text	3	000	Yes (Duplicates)
	cID	Text	4	LL00	Yes (Duplicates)
	tDate	Date	Short Date		Yes (Duplicates)

validation rule for the table. When a table is open in design view, the validation rule property can be accessed by clicking on the properties icon on the toolbar or selecting `Properties` from the `View` menu. Consider a more complicated definition of an employee table that includes an ID for the immediate supervisor of an employee. An example of a validation rule for this extended `employee` table would check that the employee's ID and the supervisor's ID are not equal, since an employee cannot be his or her own supervisor.

Referential integrity between tables is defined graphically in Access using the relationships window. To define relationships, open the `Relationships` window by selecting it as an option of the `Tools` menu. Add the tables to the relationships window display. Then, select the primary key of a table, and drag it to the table where it appears as a foreign key. At this point, a pop-up window appears. Access infers the `Relationship Type` or cardinality ratio of the relationship, based on the table and field definitions. For example, the relationship type for the referential integrity between `employee.eID` and `takes.eID` is `One-to-Many`, since one employee ID can appear many times in the `takes` table. Check the `Enforce Referential Integrity` box if you want Access to automatically enforce this relationship. When checked, Access will not allow a tuple to exist in the table if the foreign key attribute values do not refer to a valid primary key value.

As a database designer, you must also decide whether you want updates or deletes of the primary key cascaded to the records in which it appears as a foreign key. Check `Cascade Update Related Fields` if the foreign key should be updated automatically on an update of the primary key. For example, an update of the `aID` field of the `technologyArea` table should be automatically reflected in the `areaID` fields of the related `trainingCourse` records. If a record containing a primary key is deleted, check `Cascade Delete Related Records` if the related records in the table in which the value appears as a foreign key should be automatically deleted. The decision to automatically delete records should be carefully considered. You may want to define other steps for the application to take under this situation. By not checking the cascade delete box, Access will not allow a record to be deleted if there exists related records.

Figure 7.2 shows the relationships window for the EMPLOYEE TRAINING schema. To see the definition associated with a relationship, select the relationship edge graphically and then select `Edit Relationship` from the `Relationships` menu or from the menu generated by clicking the right mouse button.

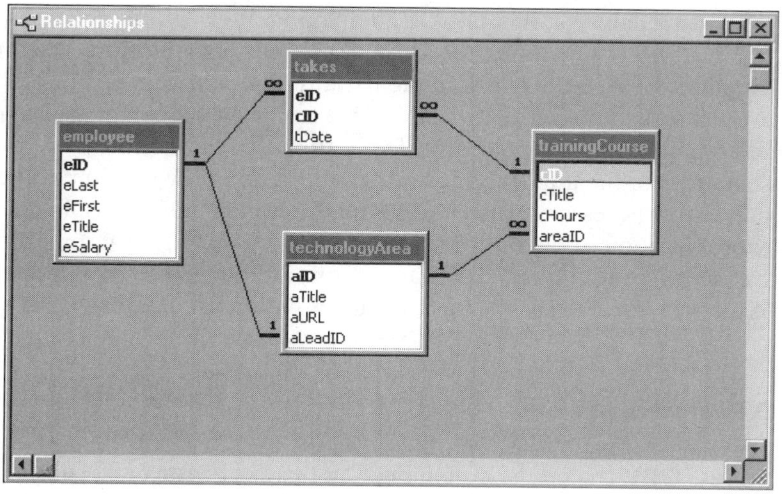

Figure 7.2 EMPLOYEE TRAINING relationships in Access.

7.2 DATA POPULATION

Obviously, once defined, the database must be populated before it can be queried. Access provides a *datasheet* view for population, which resembles a familiar spreadsheet. Figure 7.3 shows the datasheet view for the `technologyArea` table. When data are input in a datasheet view, the constraints inherently defined in the database are enforced, including any input masks, field validation rules, and referential integrity constraints.

The enforcement of referential integrity constraints implies an ordering on the population of the tuples in the tables. For example, when entering a tuple in the technologyArea : Table

Technology Area ID	Title	URL	Employee Lead
DB	Database	http://www.company.intranet/technology/db	321
JA	Java	http://www.company.intranet/technology/java	333
SE	Software Engineering	http://www.company.intranet/technology/software	345
WW	Web	http://www.company.intranet/technology/web	369

Record: 4 of 4

Figure 7.3 Table `technologyArea` datasheet view.

`technologyArea` table, the value of the `aLeadID` attribute must appear as the value of an `eID` in `employee`. There must be a valid `aID` value in the `technologyArea` table that corresponds to the `areaID` value specified in the `trainingCourse` table. Similarly, to add a record to the `takes` table requires that the corresponding `employee` and `trainingCourse` records already exist in those tables.

The sample Microsoft Access database for the EMPLOYEE TRAINING enterprise that is available at this book's companion Web site is not a complete database application. It illustrates the data definition, example instance, and querying capabilities of Access. A full implementation would also include forms and reports. Access provides wizards to help define forms, which are graphical displays that are integrated into the application for data insertion, modification, and deletion. The semantics of the application is integrated in the coordination of the forms. Reports are also a necessary part of a complete implementation, allowing for a readable representation of data in a printed format. Details of forms and reports are beyond the scope of this query language book, although the queries that one defines in Access can be used as the basis for information used in forms and reports.

7.3 ACCESS QBE

Access QBE is a GUI for defining Queries By Example (QBE). To design a query, open a new query window in design view. The query design window consists of two parts: an upper display subwindow for adding tables and join specifications and a lower field subwindow for specifying constraints on the fields for the query.

Figure 7.4 illustrates the query design for Q1, which finds the courses in the database technology area. The tables needed to answer the query are first added to the display subwindow. For Q1, tables `technologyArea` and `trainingCourse` are needed. Any relationships previously defined between the added tables specify a default equality join of the related fields when added to a query design. In Q1, there is an equality join specified between `technologyArea.aID` and `trainingCourse.areaID`.

Once the necessary tables are added to the display subwindow of the query design window, the next step is to specify attributes in the field subwindow that must be restricted in the query or projected in the query result. Attributes can be included in the field subwindow either by double clicking the mouse button while the cursor is

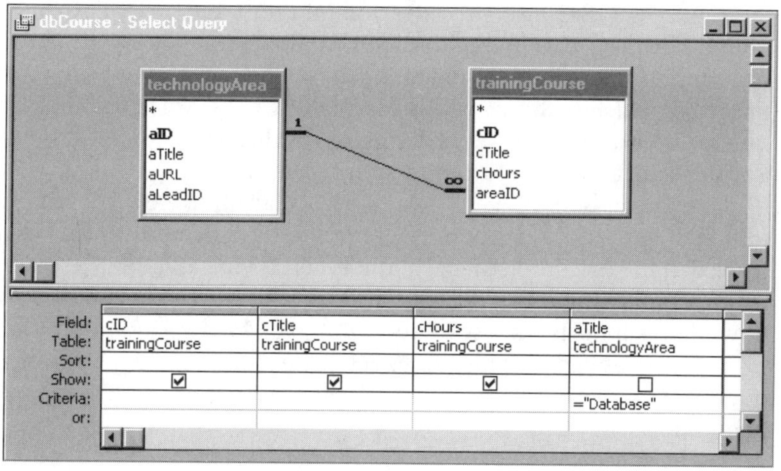

Figure 7.4 Query Q1 design view.

on the field or by selecting the field and dragging it to the field subwindow. For query Q1, the attributes `cID`, `cTitle` and `cHours` of the `trainingCourse` table form the schema of the query result, and the `aTitle` attribute of the `technologyArea` table must be restricted to select the database technology area, which is selected by the following `Criteria` specification:

```
=''Database''
```

The inclusion of an attribute in the field subwindow automatically checks the `Show` box, which indicates that the attribute is to be shown in the query result. The `Show` box for the `aTitle` field is cleared, because the attribute is not part of the result schema of the query. To run a query, select the ! from the toolbar, which automatically switches to the query's `Datasheet View` that displays the results of the query. Figure 7.5 displays the `Datasheet View` of query Q1, which shows the courses in the database technology area. Note that the headers for the fields shown in the result are the captions defined for that field during data definition.

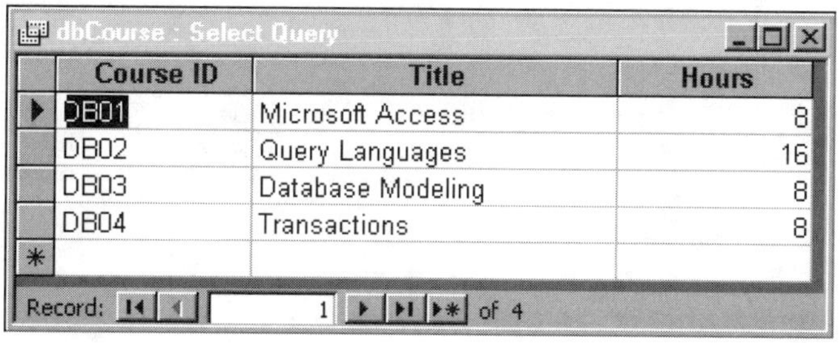

dbCourse : Select Query

Course ID	Title	Hours
DB01	Microsoft Access	8
DB02	Query Languages	16
DB03	Database Modeling	8
DB04	Transactions	8

Record: 1 of 4

Figure 7.5 Query Q1 datasheet view.

Access QBE also provides for inherent support of sorting the results of a query. The Sort row in the lower subwindow of the query design view allows a field ordering specification of Ascending, Descending, or (not sorted). The default is unsorted, which is shown with a blank Sort field. Since the six EMPLOYEE TRAINING queries do not involve the ordering of results, an example of a query that uses the Sort specification is deferred to later in the chapter.

A query definition in Access is declaring a view or virtual table. The definition is stored, and upon reference to the named query, its definition is retrieved and executed. Since a query is a virtual table, a query can be added in the display window of a query design view. In the Show Table pop-up window that supports the selection of tables to be added to the design, Access provides a tabbed display to select from Tables, Queries, or Both tables and queries. Query Q2 illustrates the design of a query that uses another query in its definition.

The specification of query Q2, which finds the employees that took a course in the database technology area, is shown in Figure 7.6. The tables needed to answer Q2 include employee, takes and the query definition of Q1, named dbCourse. The relationship between employee.eID and takes.eID provides a default join specification between these two tables. However, the join specification between the dbCourse query and the takes table must be defined explicitly, by dragging the dbCourse.cID attribute to the takes.cID attribute. Note that any join link, defined either implicitly or explicitly, can be removed by selecting the edge between the tables denoting the join and choosing the Delete option on the Edit menu or the menu resulting from a right-mouse-button click. Since an employee can take many courses in the database technology area, duplicate tuples should be removed. The designation of the removal of duplicates is not shown graphically, but is specified explicitly by setting the Unique Values property of the query to Yes. To pop up

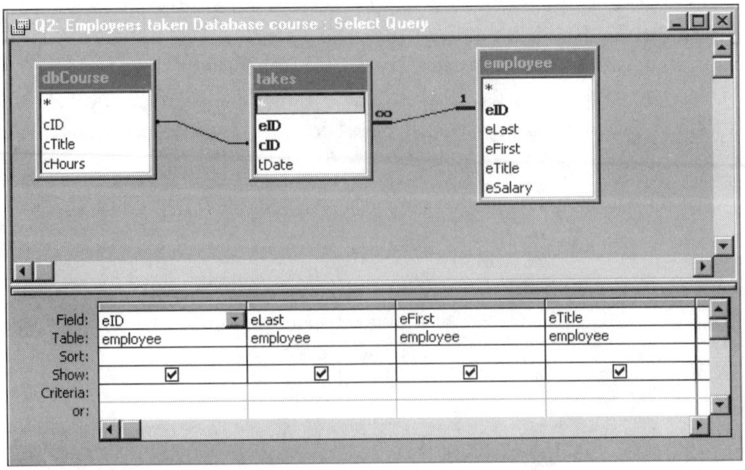

Figure 7.6 Query Q2 design view.

the query properties window, choose `Properties` on the `View` menu after selecting the query of interest, or right-click on the background of the display subwindow for the query.

Access QBE also provides support for aggregation, called *Totals*, and denoted by Σ on the query toolbar. Selecting Σ adds a `Total` row to the field subwindow of the query design window. The query Q5 that finds the employees with the minimum salary can be specified in two parts, as shown in Figure 7.7. The left query window shows the specification of query Q5i, finding the minimum employee salary by selecting the `Min` item for the `Total` of the `eSalary` attribute. The right query window joins the employee table with the query Q5i such that an employee's salary is equal to the minimum salary.

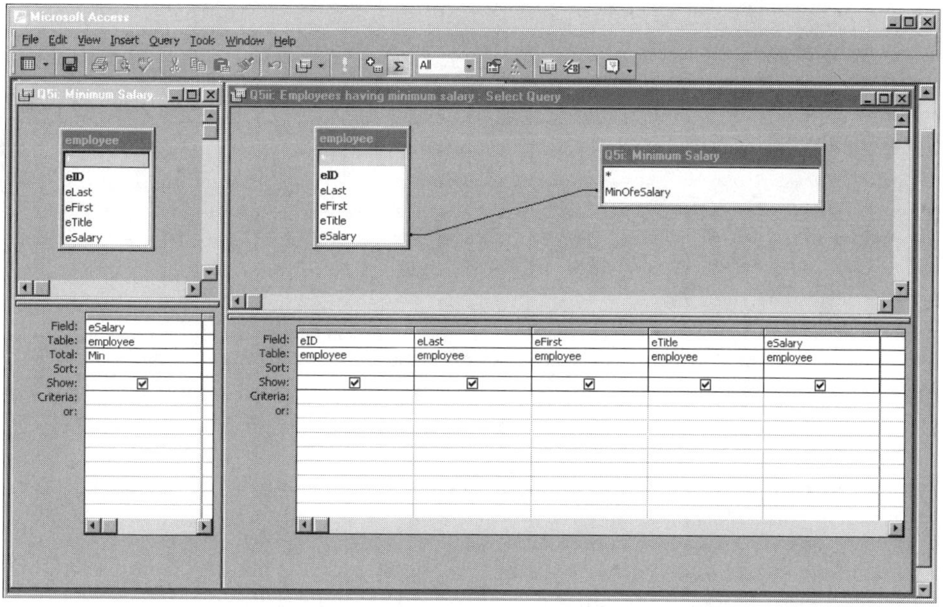

Figure 7.7 Query Q5 design view.

The query Q4 that finds the employees who took courses in more than one technology area is a little more complicated, as shown in Figure 7.8. Again, the query is specified in two parts. The first part, shown in the upper right of the query window, creates a query Q4i that finds the unique pairs of employees (`eID`) with technology areas (`areaID`) in which the employee has taken a course. Duplicate tuples must be removed for this subquery to guarantee unique pairs by setting the `Unique Values` property of the query to `Yes`. The second part of the query, shown in the left of the query window, joins the result of query Q4i with `employee` and counts the number of technology areas grouped by employee. Only those employees having more than one `areaID` are included in the query result.

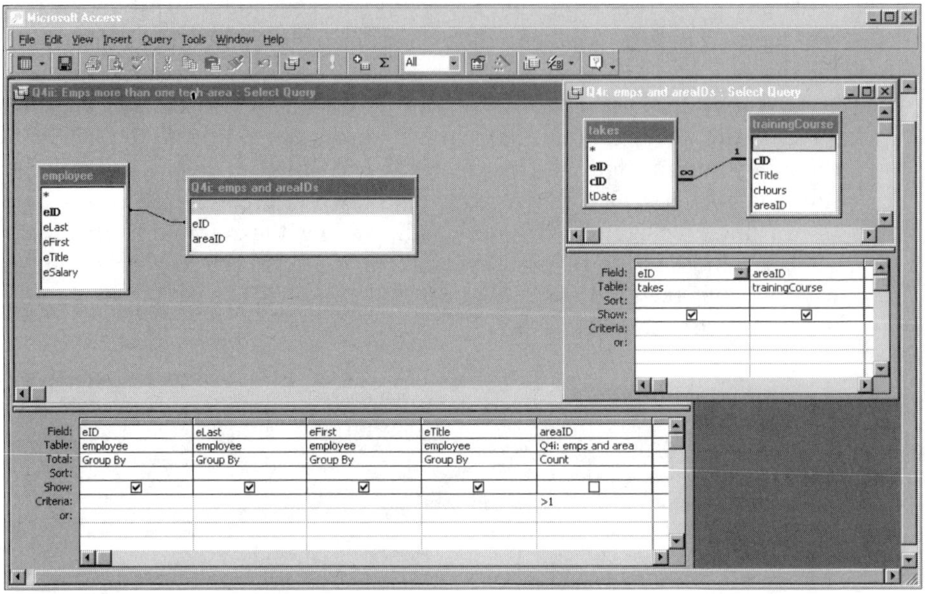

Figure 7.8 Query Q4 design view.

The example EMPLOYEE TRAINING queries Q3 and Q6 both involve negation, which is difficult to represent by example. These queries, however, can be expressed in SQL.

7.4 ACCESS SQL

Access provides support for SQL. The specifications of Q3 and Q6 from the SQL chapter work directly in Access with no changes. However, there is more to be said about SQL queries in Access.

One of the nice features of Access is that a query design specified in QBE can be easily displayed in its equivalent SQL. The `View` menu provides a choice of `Design View`, `SQL View`, and `Datasheet View`. The `Datasheet View` is the result of executing the query.

For example, consider the `SQL View` of the query Q2 for the `Design View` shown in Figure 7.6:

```
SELECT  trainingCourse.cID, trainingCourse.cTitle,
                  trainingCourse.cHours
FROM    technologyArea INNER JOIN trainingCourse
                  ON technologyArea.aID = trainingCourse.areaID
WHERE   (((technologyArea.aTitle)="Database"));
```

Access accepts the SQL-92 joined table specification in the `from` clause, joining `technologyArea` with `trainingCourse` on the related fields.[1]

It is also possible to use SQL as subqueries in conjunction with QBE. Consider the query Q3 that finds employees who have not taken any training courses:

```
select E.eID, E.eLast, E.eFirst, E.eTitle
from   employee E
where  not exists
       (select  *
       from     takes T
       where    T.eID=E.eID);
```

Figure 7.9 shows the QBE window for Q3 that uses a calculated field, named `TakenCourse`, that consists of an exists subquery having the criterion specification of `False`. The subquery could also have been specified as a `not exists` with a `True` criterion, as in the foregoing SQL specification of Q3.

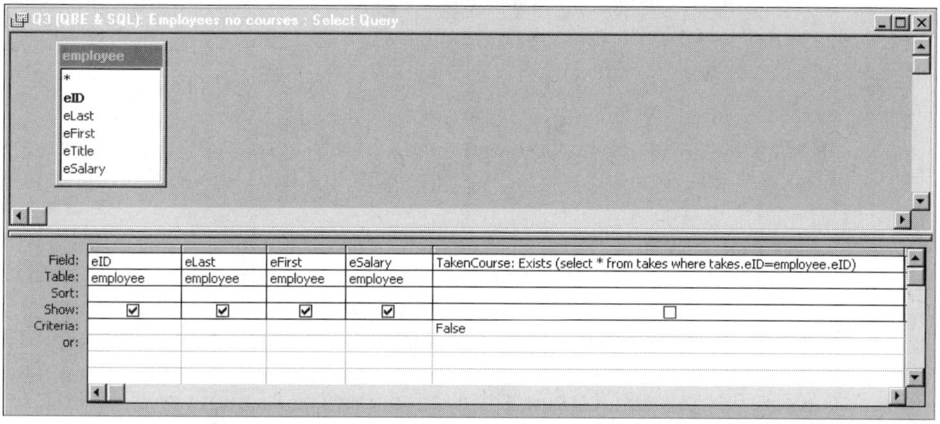

Figure 7.9 Query Q3 design view.

The `Sort` row of the QBE design window translates to an `order by` clause in its equivalent SQL. Recall the query O2 that displays the titles of employees in ascending (alphabetical) order and within that displays the salaries of the employees with the same title in descending order:

```
SELECT employee.eTitle, employee.eSalary
FROM employee
ORDER BY employee.eTitle, employee.eSalary DESC;
```

[1]SQL provides for other types of joins involving null values that are beyond the scope of this book. The keyword `INNER` denotes the familiar join, which only includes rows where the joined fields from both tables are equal.

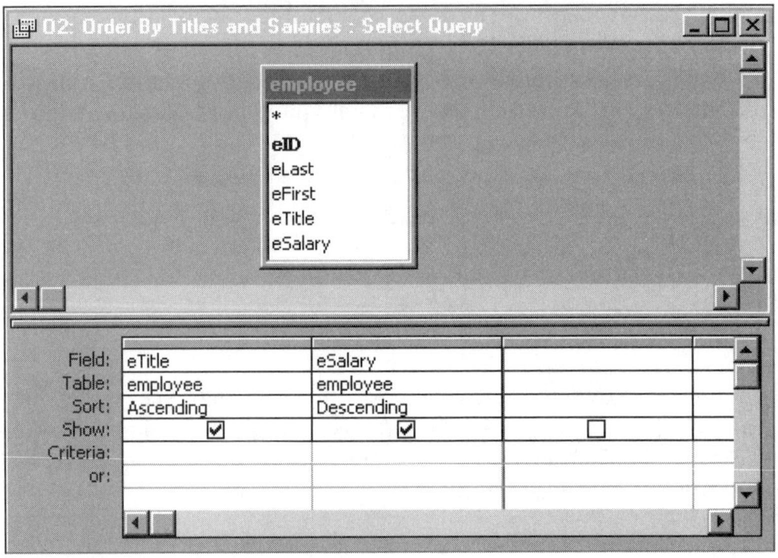

Figure 7.10 Query O2 design view.

Since the ascending sort order is the default, the explicit `ASC` specification is optional and is not shown in the preceding equivalent SQL. The QBE design of query O2 is shown in Figure 7.10.

The `Query` menu also provides an item choice of `SQL Specific`, which allows for a `Union`, `Pass-through`, or `Data Definition` query. The `Union` query allows for the standard `union` and `union all` syntax in SQL for specifying a union operation. A `Pass-through` query does not operate on the current Access database, but passes the query through to a different database source using the Open DataBase Connectivity (ODBC) standard. A `Data Definition` query allows for the creation of a table using SQL syntax instead of the graphical user interface.

7.5 ADDITIONAL FEATURES OF ACCESS QBE

The six queries over the EMPLOYEE TRAINING enterprise are called *select* queries in Access, since each select query corresponds to an SQL select statement. Recall that a select query definition in Access is defining a virtual table, which is materialized upon referencing the query name. Access QBE also provides insert, append, update, and delete capabilities.

A make-table query creates a new table and inserts the results of the query into the new table. The make-table query corresponds to an intermediate table. When the make-table query definition is executed, the tuples are materialized and inserted into the named table.

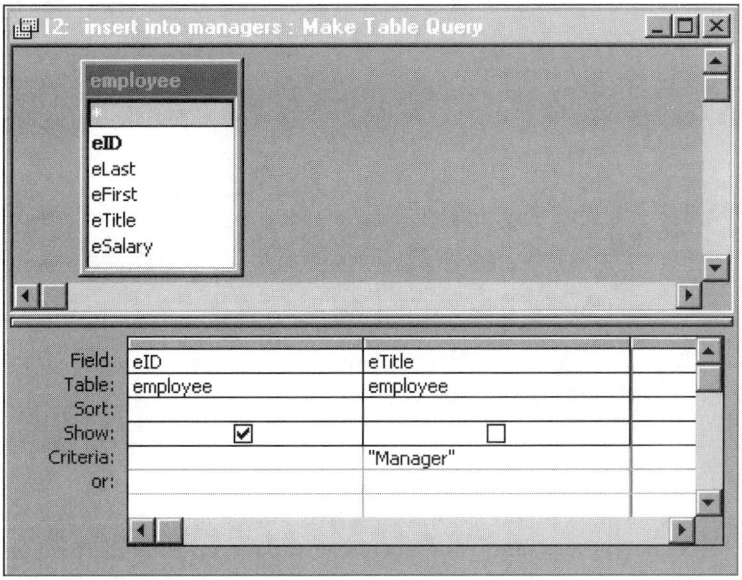

Figure 7.11 Query I2 design view.

When designing a new make-table query, Access opens a window prompting for the table name to be created in your choice of the current database or another specified database. Figure 7.11 shows the `Design View` of the Access QBE specification for the SQL `insert into` example I2 that inserts the ID of employees with the title 'Manager' into a `managers` table. To view the tuples to be inserted before executing the query, choose the `Datasheet View` of the make-table query. The `SQL View` displays the SQL that corresponds to the `Design View` of the query:

```
SELECT employee.eID INTO managers
FROM employee
WHERE (((employee.eTitle)="Manager"));
```

Once the query is designed and saved, the name of the table to be created can be revised by opening the Properties menu for the query and updating the `Destination Table` name.

An append query is similar to a make-table query, except that the tuples are appended to an existing, named table instead of creating a new table instance.

An Access QBE update query corresponds to an SQL update statement. Figure 7.12 illustrates the Access QBE definition of the SQL update example U1 that updates the salaries of employees that lead technology areas by 3%. The `employee` and `technologyArea` tables displayed in the query design window show a default join using the previously defined relationship. The `eSalary` attribute of `employee` is included in the lower window. The `Update to` row increases the

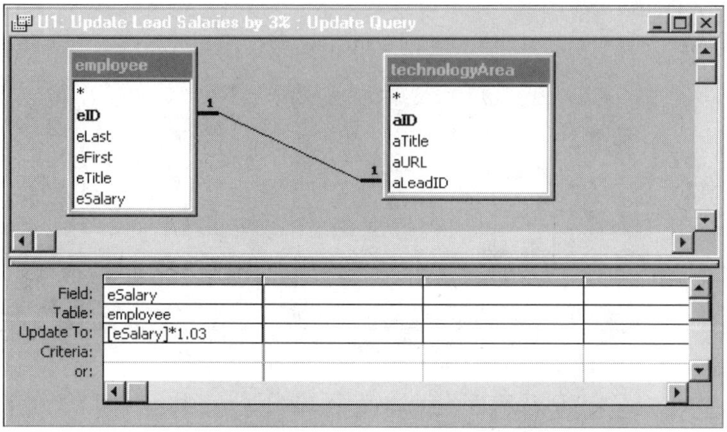

Figure 7.12 Query U1 Design View.

employee's salary by 3%. Since Access allows spaces in (table and) field names, a reference to a field name in Access is enclosed in square brackets, (e.g., `[eSalary]`). Choose the `Datasheet View` of the update query to view the salaries to be updated before executing the query. Choose the `SQL View` to see the corresponding SQL:

```
UPDATE employee INNER JOIN technologyArea
ON employee.eID = technologyArea.aLeadID
SET employee.eSalary = [eSalary]*1.03;
```

The delete query in Access QBE graphically defines a query to delete tuples from a table. For example, Figure 7.13 displays the delete query window for the

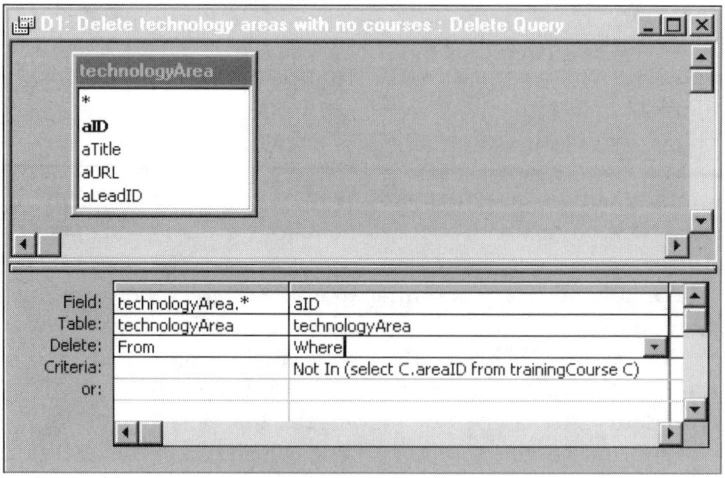

Figure 7.13 Query D1 design view.

QBE specification of the SQL `delete from` example D1 that deletes tuples from the `technologyArea` table when there are no corresponding training courses. To delete tuples from a table, add the table to the display and then include the distinguished * field in the lower window. The `Delete` row defaults to the value `From`. This incomplete specification of the delete query would delete all `technologyArea` tuples. To specify a `where` condition on the delete, include the attributes involved in the condition in the lower window: Choose the `Where` item for the `Delete` row and specify the appropriate `Criteria` for deletion. To view the tuples to be deleted before executing the query, choose the `Datasheet View` of the delete query. To see the corresponding SQL,[2] choose the `SQL View`:

```
DELETE technologyArea.*, technologyArea.aID
FROM technologyArea
WHERE (((technologyArea.aID)
           Not In (select C.areaID from trainingCourse C)));
```

The Access QBE and Access SQL languages provide a powerful capability for manipulating the database. However, these languages are not computationally complete programming languages. Therefore, Access allows for the incorporation of modules written in the Visual Basic programming language. Some examples of the capabilities provided by the use of Visual Basic include creating your own functions, performing system-level actions, and manipulating records one at a time.

7.6 SUMMARY

The query capabilities of Access are intuitive, integrating a straightforward graphical user interface QBE with the familiarity of SQL for specifying various types of queries, including select, insert (make table), append, update, and delete. A select query definition corresponds to defining a view, where the tuples are materialized for the query each time its name is referenced. A make-table query is analogous to an intermediate table, materializing the tuples to be inserted in the table once when the query definition is executed.

Common to all graphical query specifications is the upper display window where the tables involved in the query are added to the display, and the default join specifications of the tables are shown based on the defined relationships between the tables. Fields of interest to the query are included in the lower window of the design view either by double-clicking on the field or by selecting the field and dragging it to the lower window. The query properties of a field include a selection criterion for specifying a condition on the field, a `Show` box to include the field in the query result, and a sort specification for a shown field. An attractive feature of Access is the ability to switch between the various views of a query: a graphical QBE `Design`

[2]Since this SQL specification executes correctly, the attributes specified following the `delete` keyword and preceding the `from` clause do not cause any execution issues.

View, a corresponding SQL View, and a Datasheet View. The datasheet view of a select query shows the results of executing the query. Before selecting ! to run a make-table, append, update, or delete query, the datasheet view shows the potential records to be affected when the manipulation query is executed.

Although Access QBE and Access SQL provide a powerful capability for manipulating the database, Access allows for the incorporation of modules written in Visual Basic.

EXERCISES

√ Use Microsoft Access to *check* the answers to these marked exercises.

√7.1 Answer the following queries in Access over the EMPLOYEE TRAINING schema:

```
employee(eID, eLast, eFirst, eTitle, eSalary)
technologyArea(aID, aTitle, aURL, aLeadID)
trainingCourse(cID, cTitle, cHours, areaID)
takes(eID, cID, tDate)
```

An Access mdb file for the EMPLOYEE TRAINING enterprise is available at this book's companion Web site. Try to express the query using Access QBE. Use SQL only if you cannot answer the query in QBE. Verify your results against your WinRDBI solutions generated from earlier chapters:

(a) Answer the queries of Exercise 2.1.
(b) Answer the queries of Exercise 3.1.
(c) Answer the queries of Exercise 4.1.
(d) Answer the queries of Exercise 5.1.

√7.2 Consider one of the case studies from Chapter 6. Using Microsoft Access, define the database schema, including tables and relationships. Populate the database. Answer the following queries in Access QBE; use Access SQL only when necessary:

(a) WEB PAGE: Queries in Table 6.3 and Exercise 6.1.
(b) NEW HOME: Queries in Table 6.6 and Exercise 6.2.
(c) INVESTMENT PORTFOLIO: Queries in Table 6.9 and Exercise 6.3.

√7.3 Write the following operations in Access QBE over the EMPLOYEE TRAINING schema:

(a) Create a table of employees that have taken a training course in the 'Java' technology area.
(b) Modify the lead for the 'Database' technology area.
(c) Remove the training courses that are not taken by any employees.

Appendix A

WinRDBI

A.1 OVERVIEW

Relational databases are the focus of most introductory courses on database management systems. An important component of such a course is the study of query languages for retrieving information stored in a relational database. Understanding the formal relational query languages (relational algebra, DRC, and TRC) is essential to comprehending the industry-standard relational query language SQL. As a student, it is difficult to know whether your queries expressed on paper in the formal languages are correct. As an instructor, it is often difficult to grade creative queries, especially those that have not been verified using a tool or product. The goal of the Windows Relational DataBase Interpreter (WinRDBI) educational tool is to provide a mechanism by which the students can explore the formal relational query languages in an interactive environment.

WinRDBI has an intuitive GUI, as shown in Figure A.1, and runs on the Windows platform[1]. WinRDBI has the capability to graphically define a database schema and populate the tables. The student can than choose one of the following languages in which to pose queries: relational algebra, DRC, TRC, and SQL. The inclusion of the industry standard query language SQL in WinRDBI increases the usability of the educational tool, providing the ability to pose SQL queries over the same database schema and instance used for exploring the formal query languages.

WinRDBI is available for educational use at the following web site:

`http://www.eas.asu.edu/~winrdbi/`

[1]There are plans to provide WinRDBI for the Linux platform, too.

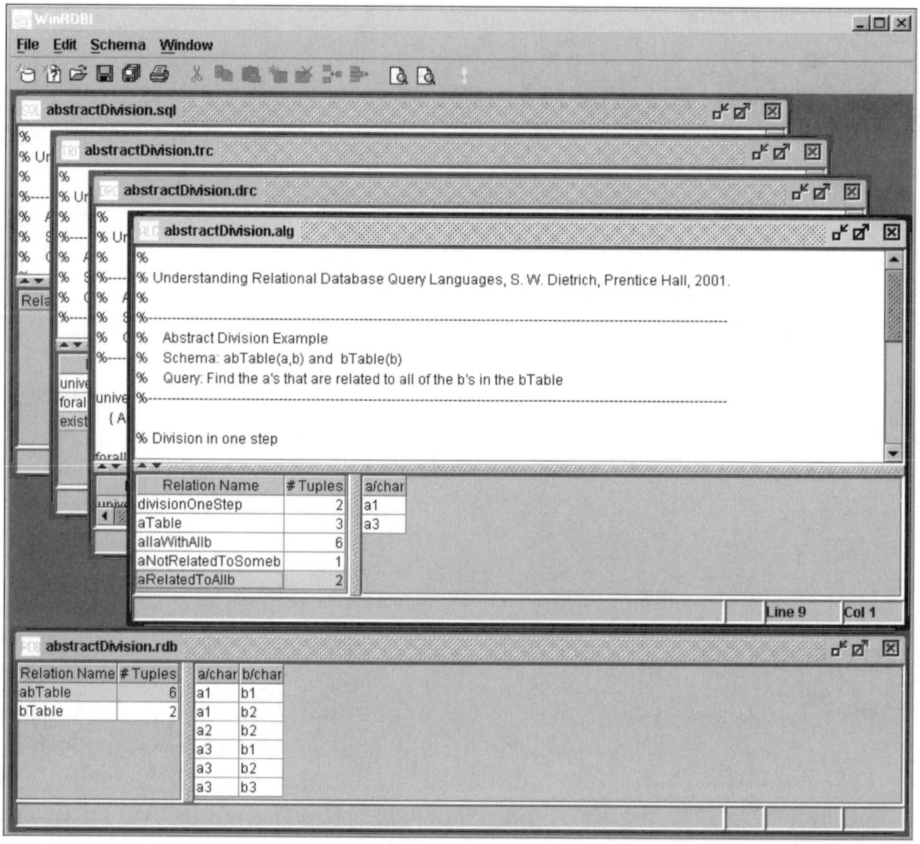

Figure A.1 WinRDBI user interface.

This book's companion web site is

`http://www.prenhall.com/dietrich/`

and includes the following for use with the WinRDBI educational tool:

- Employee Training database instance and queries in all four languages.
- Abstract division example queries in all four languages.
- Database instance and queries in all four languages for the Web Page, New Home, and Investment Portfolio case studies.

It also includes the Employee Training database instance and queries in Microsoft Access.

A.2 QUERY LANGUAGES

WinRDBI recognizes relational algebra, DRC, TRC, and SQL. The syntax of the query languages recognized by the tool is essentially the syntax presented in the chapter coverage, except for relational algebra. Since the formal syntax of relational algebra uses symbols that are not available on a computer keyword, the syntax of relational algebra recognized by WinRDBI introduces keywords in place of the symbols. This appendix provides brief coverage of any assumptions made by the WinRDBI-specific implementation of the query languages, while the WinRDBI Web page and distribution include an on-line user guide that covers the educational tool in more detail, including the user interface.

INTERMEDIATE TABLES AND RENAMING OF ATTRIBUTES

The syntax introduced for creating intermediate tables and renaming of attributes in this book is the syntax recognized by WinRDBI, where

```
intermediateTable(attr1, ..., attrn) := queryExpression;
```

assigns the result of the `queryExpression` to the `intermediateTable`, renaming the output schema of `queryExpression` to the schema given by the attribute list `attr1, ..., attrn`. If no explicit attribute list is specified, then the attribute names for the schema of `intermediateTable` are derived from the `queryExpression`.

RELATIONAL ALGEBRA

The mapping of the formal relational algebra symbols to the keywords in WinRDBI is shown in Table A.1 for the fundamental operators (σ, π, $\cup$, $-$, $\times$) and Table A.2 for the additional operators ($\cap$, $\bowtie_\theta$, $\bowtie$, $\div$).

TABLE A.1 WinRDBI summary of fundamental relational algebra operators.

Formal Relational Algebra	WinRDBI Relational Algebra
σ_θ(r)	`select θ (r)`
π_A(r)	`project A (r)`
r ∪ s	`r union s`
r − s	`r difference s`
q × r	`q product r`

TABLE A.2 WinRDBI summary of additional relational algebra operators.

Formal Relational Algebra	WinRDBI Relational Algebra
$r \cap s$	`r intersect s`
$r \bowtie_\theta s$	NOT AVAILABLE BY DESIGN
$r \bowtie s$	`njoin`
$q \div r$	NOT AVAILABLE BY DESIGN

The WinRDBI-specific assumptions for the relational algebra operators are summarized here:

- The union, difference, and intersect operators require that the operand relations be compatible by having identical schemas.
- The (Cartesian) product operator requires that the operand relations have disjoint attribute names.
- The njoin (natural join) operator does *not* require common attribute names in the operand relations. If the operand relations do not have any attribute names in common, then the natural join results in a Cartesian product.
- The theta-join and division operators are purposely not provided by the interpreter, so that students investigate the equivalent definitions of these operators in terms of the fundamental relational algebra operators.

RELATIONAL CALCULUS

Since there are many variations on the syntax of the relational calculus languages, the relational calculus chapters covered the syntax recognized by WinRDBI. The chapter examples, by convention, chose to limit a variable before its use in the query. Although this convention is not required theoretically (e.g., a conjunction is commutative), a variable must have a binding before its value is referenced in WinRDBI's left-to-right evaluation of a calculus expression.

Domain Relational Calculus. As an example in DRC, consider the specification of the Q_σ query that finds the employees who earn more than $100000:

```
{ EID, ELast, EFirst, ETitle, ESalary |
    employee(EID, ELast, EFirst, ETitle, ESalary) and
    ESalary > 100000 };
```

This specification is correct in WinRDBI, since the reference to the `employee` table binds the variable `ESalary` before checking that its value is greater than 100,000.

Another assumption in DRC is the derived schema for the result of a query expression. The DRC expression denotes the schema of the resulting query expression by listing the domain variables to the left of the vertical bar (|). Since domain variables must be identifiers starting with an uppercase letter and attribute names must be identifiers starting with a lowercase letter, WinRDBI automatically converts the DRC variable to its lowercase representation for deriving the schema for a query expression. The specification of an intermediate table with an explicit schema is strongly suggested for DRC queries that will be referenced in subsequent queries.

Tuple Relational Calculus. The only language-specific assumption for TRC is the assumed left-to-right evaluation of a TRC expression, so a tuple variable must be bound before referencing the value of any of its attributes. Consider the TRC specification of Q_σ

```
{ E | employee(E) and E.eSalary > 100000 };
```

where the value of the tuple variable `E` is bound to the `employee` table before checking that the value of the `eSalary` attribute is greater than 100000.

SQL

The syntax of the WinRDBI implementation of SQL is that of the original SQL-89 standard for the query language only.[2] Since WinRDBI has a GUI for defining and manipulating the database, the DDL and DML (insert, update, and delete) of SQL are not supported.

In addition to the basic `select-from-where` query expression, WinRDBI handles grouping, aggregation, having, order by, and nested subqueries. The interpreter, however, assumes that a nested subquery cannot involve aggregation. Aggregation must appear in the outermost query. This is not a severe restriction. The user need only break such a query into multiples queries. For example, consider the query Q5 that finds the employees earning the minimum salary over the EMPLOYEE TRAINING database:

```
select  E.eID, E.eLast, E.eFirst, E.eTitle
from    employee E
where   E.eSalary =
        (select  min(S.eSalary)
        from     employee S );
```

This formulation uses the inherent support of aggregation in SQL to compare the salary of an employee with the minimum salary found by a nested subquery. Since the tool does not allow aggregation in a nested subquery, the following two queries find the employees having the minimum salary:

[2]The SQL component of the educational tool was originally written in 1990 using C. J. Date's *A Guide to the SQL Standard*, 2nd edition, Addison Wesley, 1989 as a reference.

```
minimumSalary(minSalary) :=
        select  min(E.eSalary)
        from    employee E;

select  E.eID, E.eLast, E.eFirst, E.eTitle
from    employee E
where   E.eSalary = (select minSalary from minimumSalary);
```

A.3 IMPLEMENTATION OVERVIEW

WinRDBI is founded on the basis of established deductive database technology that uses a logic language to query the database instance stored as logical facts and the use of the Java Swing API for creating GUIs.

Prolog is used as the underlying logic language. Specifically, WinRDBI utilizes the Amzi! Prolog and Logic Server (http://www.amzi.com) to coordinate the actions specified in the GUI. Figure A.2 shows the architecture of WinRDBI. The

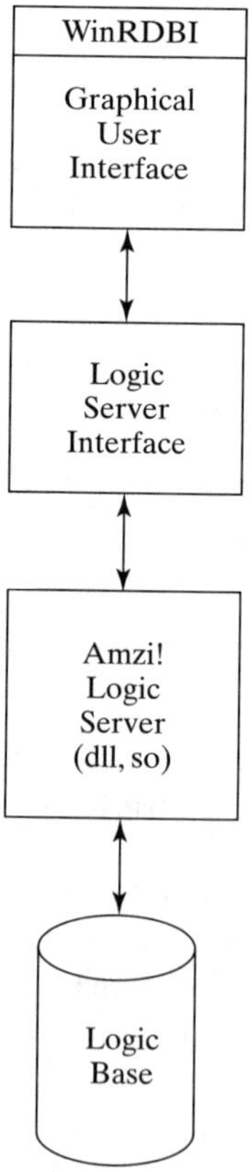

Figure A.2 WinRDBI software architectural design.

Logic Server Interface is a component of WinRDBI introduced to provide an abstraction layer between the WinRDBI user interface and the Java language bindings for the Amzi! Logic Server API (LSAPI). Amzi! was chosen for the implementation of WinRDBI, due to its features and royalty-free run-time distribution for Windows (95/98, NT, 2000), Linux, Solaris and HP/UX.[3]

The WinRDBI user interface consists of one *schema* pane and any number of *query* panes. A query pane is associated with exactly one query language. The database schema and instance shown in the schema pane is stored in Prolog during execution, but persists by saving the database instance to a file with the extension .rdb, which can be opened in a later WinRDBI session. When a query pane is selected and executed, the sequence of queries specified in a query pane is translated to Prolog code and then invoked. Since the result of a query is itself a relation, the result relations for a query pane are also stored as Prolog facts and are displayed in the lower portion of the query pane. If a named intermediate table is not explicitly created for a query, WinRDBI assigns a unique name consisting of the string `unnamed_` with a counter value appended to the end of the string.

A.4 SUMMARY

The WinRDBI educational tool is an integral component of database education at Arizona State University, providing a hands-on approach to understanding (both learning and reviewing) the capabilities of query languages for relational databases.

Although the tool is mature, future versions of WinRDBI are expected. Besides maintaining WinRDBI with respect to new releases of the Java Foundation Classes, future plans include revising SQL to be compatible with the SQL-92 standard and introducing a by-name DRC-like language.

[3] Amzi! Prolog + Logic Server is free for personal use.

Bibliographic Notes

THE RELATIONAL DATA MODEL AND FORMAL QUERY LANGUAGES

The foundation of the relational data model was first introduced in 1970 by Codd, along with the relational algebra language. Codd also defined (tuple) relational calculus and its equivalence with relational algebra in 1972. Lacroix and Pirotte described domain relational calculus in 1977. Ullman's text provides a formal proof on the equivalence of relational algebra with safe DRC and safe TRC.

- E. Codd. A relational model of data for large shared data banks. *Communications of the ACM*, 13(6):377–387, 1970.
- E. Codd. Relational completeness of data base sublanguages. In *Data Base Systems*, R. Rustin (ed.), Prentice Hall, 1972, pp. 65–98.
- M. LaCroix and A. Pirotte. Domain oriented relational languages. In *Proc. of the Conf. on Very Large Databases*, 1977.
- J. Ullman. *Principles of Database and Knowledge Base Systems, Vols. 1 and 2.* Computer Science Press, 1989.

CONCEPTUAL MODELING

There are many papers on conceptual modeling for databases. Chen proposed the ER Conceptual Model in 1976, and its use in database design was formalized in 1981 by Ng. Teorey *et al* provide a design methodology for developing an ER model, which is then translated to the relational model. Although the ER conceptual data model is well established in the database community, the Unified Modeling Language (UML) standard (see Rumbaugh, Jacobson, and Booch) developed for the design of software may someday be used by database designers as well. (See Muller.) There is a high degree of similarity between conceptual modeling with ER diagrams and the conceptual class diagrams of UML.

- P. P. Chen. The entity-relational model–toward a unified view of data. *ACM Transactions on Database Systems*, 1(1):9–36, 1976.
- R. J. Muller. *Database Design for Smarties: Using UML for Data Modeling.* Morgan Kaufmann, 1999.
- P. Ng. Further analysis of the Entity-Relationship Approach to Database Design. *IEEE Transactions on Software Engineering*, 7:1, 1981.
- J. Rumbaugh, I. Jacobson, and G. Booch. *The Unified Modeling Language Reference Manual.* Addison Wesley, 1998.
- T. Teorey, D.-Q. Yang, and J. Fry. A logical database design methodology for relational databases using the extended entity-relationship model. *ACM Computing Surveys*, 18(2):197–222, 1986.

DEDUCTIVE DATABASES

The DRC language is related to the Datalog language of deductive databases, which is a field of study emphasizing the use of a language based on logic to query the database instance stored as logical facts. The Datalog language looked similar to the Prolog (Programming in Logic) language, which was developed in the early 1970's, but the evaluation of the languages were significantly different. Whereas Prolog assumed a particular strategy for the evaluation of the language, the goal of Datalog was to declaratively specify queries in logic and let the database system have the responsibility to determine an efficient evaluation of the declarative query. (Clocksin and Mellish is a classic Prolog text, and Maier and Warren provide a database perspective in their book on computing with logic.) There are several collections that chronicle the research and applications of deductive databases. (See Gallaire and Minker 1978, Minker 1988, and Ramakrishnan 1995.) The 1980's saw the development of numerous deductive database prototypes, which are recently surveyed in 1995 by Ramakrishnan and Ullman. In the 1990's, a commercial product, called VALIDITY (see Vieille), was developed by Bull Worldwide Information Systems and later by Next Century Media, Inc., that integrates a declarative language for the flexibility of specifying business rules with an imperative language similar to C++ (See Friesen *et al.*) The DRC by-name syntax presented in Chapter 3 is reminiscent of the syntax used in VALIDITY's declarative language, called Datalog Extended Language (DEL). There are also several textbooks available that provide coverage of deductive databases. (See Abiteboul *et al*, Ceri *et al*, and Ullman.) Recently, as indicated by the VALIDITY system, the emphasis in this area has been the integration of objects and rules. (See Ceri and Fraternali, which also includes a chapter on VALIDITY.)

- S. Abiteboul, R. Hull and V. Vianu. *Foundations of Databases*. Addison Wesley, 1995.
- S. Ceri and P. Fraternali. *Designing Database Applications with Objects and Rules*. Addison Wesley, 1997.
- S. Ceri, G. Gottlob, and L. Tanca. *Logic Programming and Databases*. Springer-Verlag, 1990.
- W. F. Clocksin and C. S. Mellish. *Programming in Prolog*, 4th edition. Springer Verlag, 1994.
- O. Friesen, G. Gauthier-Villars, A. Lefebvre, and L. Vieille, Applications of Deductive-Object Databases using DEL, In *Applications of Logic Databases*, R. Ramakrishnan (ed.) Kluwer Academic, Boston, MA, 1995.
- H. Gallaire and J. Minker. *Logic and Databases*. Plenum Press, 1978.
- D. Maier and D. S. Warren. *Computing with Logic: Logic Programming with Prolog*. Benjamin Cummings, 1988.
- J. Minker (ed.). *Foundations of Deductive Databases and Logic Programming*. Morgan Kaufmann, 1988.
- R. Ramakrishnan. *Applications of Logic Databases*. Kluwer Academic, Boston, MA, 1995.
- R. Ramakrishnan and J. Ullman. A survey of deductive database systems. *Journal of Logic Programming*, 23(2):125–149, 1995.
- J. Ullman. *Principles of Database and Knowledge Base Systems, Vols. 1 and 2*. Computer Science Press, 1989.
- L. Vieille. From Data Independence to Knowledge Independence: An on-going story. In *Proceedings of the Very Large Data Base Conference*, 1998.

SQL

SQL is *the* industry-standard query language. SQL is based on SEQUEL, which was introduced in the mid-1970's as the query language for IBM's System R project. (See Boyce and Chamberlin and Chamberlin *et al.*) The original SQL standard was ratified in 1986 by the American National Standards Institute (ANSI) and is informally referred to as SQL-86. The International Standards Organization (ISO) accepted the ANSI standard as an international standard in 1987. This standard was extended to include an integrity enhancement feature in 1989 and is informally referred to as SQL-89. The SQL-92 standard added many features that include explicit support of intersect, except, and join, as well as embedded SQL, to name a few. Melton and Simon provide a readable overview of SQL-92. Although not for the novice, Date with Darwen provide a reference guide to the SQL standard. In December 1999, the latest standard SQL:1999 (http://www.ansi.org) was ratified and includes support for extended relational systems, sometimes called object-relational databases, that provide inherent support for user-defined data types and object tables (see Gulutzan and Pelzer).

- R. Boyce and D. Chamberlin. SEQUEL: a structured English query language. In *ACM SIGMOD Conf. on Management of Data*, 1974.
- D. Chamberlin, M. Astrahan, K. Eswaran, P. Griffiths, R. Lorie, J. Mehl, P. Reisner and B. Wade. Sequel 2: A unified approach to data definition, manipulation, and control. *IBM Journal of Research and Development*, 20(6):560–575, 1976.
- C. J. Date with H. Darwen. *A Guide to the SQL Standard, 4th edition*. Addison Wesley, 1997.
- P. Gulutzan and T. Pelzer. *SQL-99 Complete, Really*. CMP Books, 1999.
- J. Melton and A. Simon. *Understanding the New SQL: A Complete Guide*. Morgan Kaufmann, 1993.

DATABASE TEXTBOOKS

This book is designed to be both a standalone introduction to the relational data model and relational query languages and a supplemental text to existing database textbooks that may not be able to cover numerous examples with an emphasis on the formal query languages.

- P. Atzeni, S. Ceri, S. Paraboschi and R. Torlone. *Database Systems Concepts, Languages and Architectures*. McGraw-Hill, 2000.
- T. Connelly, C. Begg and A. Strachan. *Database Systems - A Practical Approach to Design, Implementation, and Management*, 2nd edition. Addison-Wesley, 1999.
- R. Elmasri and S. Navathe. *Fundamentals of Database Systems, 3rd edition*. Addison Wesley, 2000.
- D. Kroenke. *Database Processing Fundamentals, Design and Implementation, 7th edition*. Prentice-Hall, 2000.
- F. R. McFadden, J. A. Hoffer and M. B. Prescott. *Modern Database Management, 5th edition*. Addison-Wesley, 1999.
- P. O'Neil and E. O'Neil. *Database Principles, Programming, and Performance*, 2nd edition. Morgan Kaufman, 2001.
- R. Ramakrishnan and J. Gehrke. *Database Management Systems*, 2nd edition. McGraw-Hill, 2000.
- A. Silberschatz, H. F. Korth, and S. Sudarshan. *Database System Concepts*, 3rd edition. McGraw-Hill, 1997.
- J. Ullman and J. Widom. *A First Course in Database Systems*. Prentice-Hall, 1997.

Index